ALCESTER
NATIONAL SCHOOLS
1871 ~ 1903

To Tony
best wishes
from Karyl.

ALCESTER
NATIONAL SCHOOLS
1871 ~ 1903

KARYL REES

BREWIN BOOKS

First published by
Brewin Books Ltd, 56 Alcester Road,
Studley, Warwickshire B80 7LG in 2013
www.brewinbooks.com

ISBN: 978-1-85858-516-1

A Cataloguing in Publication Record
for this title is available from the British Library

Typeset in Minion Pro
Printed in Great Britain by
4edge Ltd.

CONTENTS

Chapter 1

INTRODUCTION

Before 1870, schooling was left to private owners or voluntary organisations – 'public' schools for the wealthy or charitable schools, usually run by Churches, for the poor. In 1811, the National Society for the Promotion of Religious Education encouraged the setting up of schools which were called National Schools. The intention was that the 'National Religion should be the basis for a National Education'. Alcester's School was inspected by HM Inspectors, reporting directly to the Privy Council. As well as receiving some grant money from the Government, schools received pupil fees and charitable donations.

By 1870 Alcester already had a National School, set up in 1843, run by the Rector and a group of subscribers who provided a minimum of 20/- (£1), which entitled them to a place on the Board of Managers, with each 10/- (50p) giving them one vote on the Board. Queen Adelaide, widow of King William IV, had given the first subscription to the School when she stayed at Ragley Hall.

The original school building was erected on land donated by Lord Hertford, on the Moors (now School Road) off Birmingham Road. The Schools were then referred to in the plural as the building was, at this time, divided into two departments – the Boys' School and the Girls' School – separated by the School House occupied by the Master. Each School had its own Head Master or Mistress, classroom, playground and entrance.

Pupils were charged fees (school pennies) and paid for their own copy books – much education being the copying down of information from a blackboard. Children did not need to attend on a full time basis – some worked for part of the day as well as attending school, and some attended school in the evenings. The Factory Act 1867 laid down that children aged between 3 and 13 were restricted to half time working, and such children should attend school for 10 hours a week until they were 13 years old.

Anyone could set up a school and teachers did not need to be qualified. Many were little more than child-minders.

The National Schools were not the only elementary schools in Alcester at the time – in 1867 it was recorded that the Newport Free School in Birch Abbey, which later became the Grammar School, had a preparatory department with 6 boys receiving free elementary education.

Map of Alcester, early 1900s.

In the 1871 census, we see Sarah Franklin running a boarding school at 21 High Street, having 9 children, both boys and girls, aged from 6 to 10 years; Mrs Elizabeth Boddington and her daughter Elizabeth ran a small school in Butter Street; Sarah Mascall's school was in Henley Street next to the Baptist Chapel; Mary Steward had a school which moved from Evesham Street to Churchill House opposite the Town Hall circa 1874; Poplar Cottage, Evesham Street housed, until 1898, a ladies' boarding school, which also took day girls, and Sarah Davis ran a school in Priory Street (now Priory Road) up to 1874.

The Forster Elementary Education Act of 1870 tried to fill in the gaps where there were no church elementary schools. This gave the Rector and Subscribers a choice. They could continue to run Alcester as a Voluntary Church School, or they could step back and allow a new school to be built in the town, run by a Board of Managers selected by the Department of Education. This would have had to be funded by extra local taxes.

To retain local control, it was decided to alter and enlarge the existing school buildings to include an Infants' department to comply with Government regulations. The Managers also decided to build two school houses on the same site – one each for the Master and Mistress. The 'new' Alcester Schools were subject to annual inspection by Her Majesty's Inspectors to qualify for a small grant, as well as inspection by the Religious Inspector for the Diocese of Worcester.

The following chapters are based on the Boys' School Logbook (1863-1890), the Infants' School Logbooks (1881-1903) and the Minutes Book of the Managers' Meetings (1871-1903). In 1903, the Schools were incorporated into the new Warwickshire Local Education Authority, while still retaining their Voluntary status as Church of England Schools.

As part of a community project set up by Alcester Heritage Network, I volunteered to transcribe these documents and set up a database of those Managers, Staff, pupils, tradesmen and visitors mentioned in the books. It turned out to be a fascinating insight, not only to the day-to-day running of the Schools with all the attendant problems and successes, but a glimpse into the way of life in a small market town in the 1800s.

Some of the problems and frustrations encountered by the teachers are familiar to me as a teacher in the 20th century, but I have great admiration for the pioneers – both teachers and Managers – who were so obviously trying their best to educate the children under difficult circumstances and with few resources.

There is a limit to what can be included – there is far more information in the original documents and the transcripts which are held by Alcester Heritage Network. [e-mail: enquiries@alcesterheritage.org.uk or tel: 07857 364383]

Direct quotations are in italics, complete with original punctuation and grammar. Some background information was found in G.E. Saville's 'Short History of Alcester's Schools 1490-1912' published by Alcester & District Local History Society in 1978. Photographs are reproduced by kind permission of Mr. J. Bunting, Mrs. P. Barry, Alcester & District Local History Society, Alcester Community Archive Collection and Alcester Heritage Network. Thanks, too, to Joy Pegrum of the Alcester Heritage Network for her support.

Chapter 2

A NEW SCHOOL

In January 1871, there was a meeting held at Alcester Town Hall:

> *'for the purpose of forming a School Committee and making arrangements for carrying out the provisions of the Elementary Education Act 1870 in the Parish of Alcester.*
>
> *The Rector in opening the proceedings explained the circumstances under which he had convened the meeting, and although under the terms of the Trust deed the school is to be under the control and management of the Rector for the time being, he desired to associate with himself in the management such persons as would be likely to take an Interest in the Education of the poor of Alcester.'*

The meeting was convened by the Rev. Alfred Henry Williams, Rector of Alcester, and attended by Thomas Lant Smith (surgeon), William Allwood (factory owner), William Grizzell (retired draper), William Williams (retail wine merchant), Rev. Moses Philpin (Baptist minister), Henry Mather, John Laughton Jones (solicitor), Thomas Averill (twine manufacturer) and John Williams (retired wine merchant).

It was resolved:

> *'that the Schools be opened on Monday Jany 9th under the new Act the funds to be under the control of the committee that the Master and Mistress be offered a fixed salary for conducting the same for a period of twelve months from the above date viz Mr Sayce Sixty pounds and Miss Walsingham Twenty pounds – in addition to which each to receive one third of the Government grant and one third of the pence earned in their respective Schools.'*

The following Gentlemen *'consented to act on the committee'* which would run the school:

Rev. A.H. Williams (Chairman), R. Fisher, Thomas Lant Smith, Henry Walker, Thomas Haywood Smith (surgeon and son of Thomas Lant Smith), John Laughton Jones, William Allwood, G. Wyman, Thomas Averill, Richard H. Harbridge (Headmaster of Birch Abbey Grammar School), W. Grizzell, A. Jackson,

John Williams, Rev. M Philpin, B Hughes and the Marquis of Hertford. Mr. T.L. Smith was appointed Treasurer and Mr. J. Williams, Secretary.

Some existing staff members were kept on. These were the Master, James Sayce, a former Butter Street confectioner then aged 57, and the Mistress, Miss Lucy Walsingham, a Government Certificated teacher aged 28 from Coughton. Pupil Teacher Samuel Hartles, aged 16, was not kept on because the Privy Council Inspection of December 1870 reported:

'Hartles – Geography History English and Arithmetic, he has failed in his examination Article 81(C) The Managers must consult clauses 3 and 5 of his Memorandum of Agreement and determine whether they will retain his services.'

Although Mr. Sayce wrote in the logbook most days when the Schools were open, many entries record 'nothing of note', and there are many where children were *'admonished for throwing stones'*, being cheeky to people passing by, loitering on the way to and from school and playing in the snow. He also records instances of fevers in the town, and the death of several children during the regular epidemics. There is little recorded about the actual teaching in the Schools. After the appointment of Rev. Alfred H. Williams as Rector of Alcester in 1869, the teaching of Scripture was more or less taken over by him.

The Government Inspector's reports on the Schools up to this time were very critical of the discipline and teaching of Mr. Sayce, which was regarded as being less than satisfactory. In September 1868 it is recorded:

'Discipline, Instruction and General Efficiency fair, Religious Knowledge, Reading and Arithmetic pretty fair, Dictation fair History of England rather moderate only the two Boys in the sixth Standard answered well in this subject and very few others in Scripture.'

Mr. Thomas Lant Smith (Treasurer).

Mr. Sayce had, up until 1870, run the Schools as he wished, and the change in requirements and the intervention of Her Majesty's Inspectorate came as a setback to his personal and financial situation. He had been in charge of distributing the money paid over by the Managers to cover staffing costs, but had not needed to account for it. His wife, Sarah, also 'taught' at the school.

The first year was a turbulent one.

In January, Mr. Sayce was told he could no longer keep for himself extra money paid by night school attendees, and had to hand over ownership of stationery, furniture and fittings to the Managers, but not without claiming a refund of costs based on his own receipts: Miss Walsingham was given three months' notice to quit. During the previous year Miss Walsingham had been absent from school on many occasions, due to ill health, and the Managers decided to employ a more robust individual.

In February, Mrs. Fanny E. Bates was appointed Mistress of the Girls' School, though she was unable to leave her existing post at Shipston-on-Stour until the end of the summer term.

March saw the Committee still coming to terms with the changes in regulations, and having to call in an architect to help plan new buildings, their own plans not being acceptable to the Education Department. Tom Colling was appointed as a pupil teacher i.e. a pupil beyond school leaving age who could serve an apprenticeship by learning in the classroom. This could lead to his becoming an Assistant and eventually a Master. He would be paid a small amount of money by the Master.

After a month without a properly appointed Mistress, though Mrs. Sayce did step in to help, Mr. Sayce wrote to the Committee asking for some recompense for extra duties.

By the end of July, the Education Department wanted room sizes on the plan to be reduced, and the Charity Commissioners became involved with appointments to the Management Committee.

In August of 1871, there was a damning report on the performance of the Schools. The Boys' School logbook records H.M. Inspector's comments:

'Discipline, Instruction & general efficiency, moderate. The senior pupil teacher [Samuel Hartles] was dismissed at the beginning of the official year as incompetent. The certificated assistant Mistress left without giving any notice in the middle of it and the Master appears to have been thoroughly overworked. He, his wife and the pupil teacher have all done their best but they have failed.

In no subject did the children come up to a fair average and the reading is particularly bad.

The Grant is reduced for one tenth article 32 (b) for faults of discipline and instruction mentioned by H.M. Inspector.

A deduction is also incurred under article 32 (c), as the school Staff has been insufficient since the departure of the Assistant Mistress to satisfy that Article.'

The Schools lost almost 20% of its Grant for the year.

In September, Mr. John Phillip of Long Compton was appointed in place of Mr. Sayce, who tendered his resignation as from the end of December. However, Mr. Sayce did not go quietly. He wrote to the Managers:

'If you will pay over to me the whole of the Government Grant received by you for the Alcester N. Schools for the last 6 months I will return to you the salary which you have paid Tom Colling to Xmas last and resign all Claims to my portion of the Government Grant which will be due to me at Xmas next.'

This implies that poor Tom had been working for nothing in the classroom, and the Managers could not understand what had happened:

'the Secretary was directed to request Mr Sayce to make known his wishes in a more intelligible shape.'

In October, Mrs. Bates told the Committee that she needed extra help to run the Girls' School. It was decided to advertise in the Alcester Chronicle and Redditch Indicator for a transfer pupil teacher. There were also questions asked in Committee about the finances, and what steps might be taken to raise money for the altering and rebuilding of the Schools.

Later in October, the Managers had to hold a special meeting to consider a charge against Mr. Sayce of taking *'indecent liberties'* and *'using obscene language'* towards one of the girls in the School. Another pupil corroborated the girl's accusation and Mr. Sayce, *'not being able to rebut'* the charge, was summarily dismissed and the Boys' School closed until further notice. The School accounts were also ordered to be examined. The Managers wrote to Mr. Sayce:

'It is the unanimous decision of the committee that the charge now preferred against you is proved and in their duty to the public they feel bound to dismiss you at once from your position as Master of the School and require you to leave the premises on or before Saturday week.'

This meant vacating the School House as well as leaving his post as Master.

At the end of the year, the main topic being discussed by the Managers was the question of raising money for the new Schools, though they were able to find seven pounds ten shillings (£7.50) to reward Mrs. Bates:

> *'for her services in conducting the Boys School during the unavoidable absence of a master. It was also agreed to give her Daughter one pound for the assistance rendered to her Mother in the same period.'*

The new Master, Mr. Phillip, took up his post in January 1872.

According to the 1881 census, Mr. Sayce was still in the town, being registered in a house in Stratford Road, Alcester. He died in 1889 aged 75. Miss Walsingham, having married joiner Mr. Joseph Peat from Derby, was living in Smalley, Derbyshire. She died in Belper, Derbyshire in 1908. Mrs Bates was still Mistress of the Girls' School, and remained there until 1899.

Chapter 3

PROGRESS

The arrival of Mr John Phillip marked an improvement in the academic achievements of the Boys' School, as Mrs. Bates' appointment had done in the Girls' School. Early entries in the logbook for 1872 mention the poor standard of children's (boys') attainments in Reading, Writing, Arithmetic and Dictation. This had also been noted by Rev. H.M. Capel, Her Majesty's Inspector for Schools, during annual inspections.

During the previous year, the Rector, Rev. Alfred H. Williams, had visited the Schools regularly in order to give Scripture lessons, and he continued to do so for some time. The Marquis of Hertford also tried to encourage the children by offering prizes for the best performances in Reading, Writing and Arithmetic. These prizes continued to be awarded until the Marquis' death in 1884. In 1887, one of his sons, Lord Ernest Seymour, offered a prize in a Writing Competition.

The first recipients of these prizes included William Bagnall, Henry Cox, William Field, Wesley Gittus, Alexander Skinner, Charles Skinner and Edwin Strain. The prize-giving continued, and in 1873, the winners were William Bagnall, Henry Biddle, James Cale, Henry Cox, Wesley Gittus, Alfred Hallam, Charles Hunt, William Hunt and John Lock.

Average weekly attendances at the beginning of 1872 were just over 50, with many children missing school in wet or snowy weather, especially those from the workhouse and part-time factory children. In January:

'Mr. Striedinger (Sub Inspector of Factories) called in the morning and again in the afternoon and on both occasions he spoke to the half timers urging them to attend regularly & punctually.'

Mr. Phillip, being also the St. Nicholas' Church organist, introduced singing lessons to the Schools, with both boys and girls learning songs together. The songs taught were typical of this era, with titles such as, 'Welcome Summer', 'The Swallows', 'Victoria the Beloved' and 'The Spring of Youth'. A school Choir was formed, and children took part in Choir festivals. This initiative is favourably recorded in the HMI Report for 1873 – *'The Singing deserves praise.'*

This Report also shows a pleasing improvement in the performance of the Master and the achievements of the children, though it is noted that:

'Mr. Phillip has an unusually large number of Half Timers, and I am sorry to say, many of these were very backward when admitted.'

Mr. Phillip tried to augment the children's part-time education with 'Home Lessons' or 'Night Lessons' but on many occasions records that these were either not done, or done very poorly, and the children concerned were kept in after school hours to re-do the work.

May 1875 shows a typical entry:

'Found it still necessary to detain a great many children after school hours on account of unpunctuality & carelessness in learning Home Lessons.'

In general, academic achievement continued to improve with a small group of boys in different Standards winning the prizes offered by Lord Hertford. The boys were classified into Standards according to ability, and taught accordingly. In January 1874 prizes were awarded to Wesley Gittus, Henry Cox and William Stanley (Standard I), Alfred Hallam and Charles Hunt (Standard II) and Albert Malins and J Cornwall (Standard III).

St Nicholas' Church, Alcester, 1879.

In July 1874, when the school was examined by Her Majesty's Inspector, the Rev. H.M. Capel, and his assistant Mr. Burridge, Wesley Gittus, Henry Cox and William Stanley were presented for an extra examination in Literature '*all of whom passed*.' Fifty other children, chosen by the Master, were examined in Reading, Writing – including dictation – and Arithmetic. The Government Grant took into account the number of passes in these subjects (Payment by Results).

The Literature examination passes earned the school 9/- (45p) extra. The Report for 1874 was as follows:

'Buildings and offices [toilets] *much improved and very good. Reading, Dictation and arithmetic pretty good. Fitness for training apprentices and general efficiency satisfactory.'*

No for Payment at 6/-	61
Qualified for Examination	63
Presented	50
Passes in Reading	41
„ „ Writing	41
„ „ Arithmetic	41
	123
No for Payment at 4/-	123
„ „ „ „ 3/- Literature	3
Amt earned on Average Attendance	£18.6.0
„ „ „ Examination	£24.12.0
„ „ „ Literature	9.0
Total Grant	£43.7.0

The Report is signed by Mr. Phillip and the Rector, Rev. Alfred H. Williams as Chairman of the Committee.

Mr. Phillip was determined to extend the syllabus of the school. As well as introducing the singing lessons, and presenting a few children for the extra Literature examination, at the end of 1875 he introduced Geography to the boys in the higher Standards, '*for which new books were purchased in Birmingham on Tuesday last.*' During the same week, he also '*Commenced teaching the children (in Standard II & upwards) Grammar.*'

To ensure success in these extra subjects, the 1st class boys were induced to attend school 15 minutes '*earlier every morning in order to take them in the extra subjects.*' During the Whitsuntide Holidays, '*most of the 1st class boys attended for an hour every morning in order to have a Geography Lesson.*'

Unfortunately, it was these boys who were of an age to leave school, and in June 1876 there were only 5 boys left in the 1st class.

All the extra work did produce results, as the end-of-year report for 1877 by Her Majesty's Inspector, Rev. H.M. Capel, shows:

'The examination, on the whole, pleased me much. The discipline is good. The Reading is very satisfactory and the Writing, Arithmetic, Grammar, and Geography very fair.'

and in 1879:

'The school continues in a satisfactory state and the work both elementary & extra gives evidence of careful grounding. The education given is thorough & useful and well suited to the class of boys attending the school.'

That same year, three children – Claude Phillip (son of the Master), Charles Bayliss and Thomas Blackband – were awarded a free scholarship to the Grammar school by means of a competitive public examination.

The results are also reflected in the larger number of children presented for examination, with 74 out of 75 passes in Reading, 62 out of 75 in Writing and 61 out of 75 in Arithmetic. This of course meant an increase in the Government Grant for that year, which was a total of £70-11-0.

The Schools usually worked to a standardised Time Table, set down by Government – similar to the National Curriculum today – but in 1878, Mr. Phillip was finding it difficult to do this because of an increase in the number of pupils, especially younger ones. The previous November he had written:

'The 4th class is now full to overflowing whilst many of the children can scarcely do anything. The Geography of the IV – VI standards proves very hard this year. Great difficulty had been experienced during the last few weeks in consequence.'

In January 1878 he wrote:

'As the attendance has increased so much of late it has been found impossible at all times to work strictly according to The Time Table. In order to meet this difficulty, until the staff is increased, a few temporary alterations have been made in the Time Table.'

At the end of February 1878, there was another reason:

'The Time Table has again been departed from & the singing lessons dispensed with on account of Miss Bates' illness.'

Her illness lasted several weeks, but there is no record of exactly when she returned, just that the singing lessons were re-commenced during the week ending 29th March.

In the Infants' School, too, after its formation in 1881, there was an 'approved list of lessons'. For 1883, the list consisted of the following:

Animals
1 The Sheep
2 The Cow
3 The Cat
4 The Elephant
5 The Camel
6 The Lion

Objects
1 Water
2 An Orange
3 Bird's Nest
4 The Clock Face
5 Finger-nails
6 Colour sheet

[Note: These same lessons were still on the 'approved list' twenty years later.]

The hard work of Mr. Phillip was paying off and after the Annual Inspection in June 1878, when the Grant went up to £81-6-0, two pupils were awarded Honour Certificates. In October:

'The Rev A H Williams attended school early in the week in order to present Claude Phillip & Charles [Bayliss] with the Honour Certificate gained by them under the 18th section of the Education Act 1876. At the same time he took the opportunity of impressing upon the other children the necessity of attending school regularly.'

Rev. Williams was very appreciative of the work done in the schools and in June 1885 it is recorded that Mr. Phillip was given, *'half holiday on Thursday to attend the Annual Treat given to Teachers & others by the Rev A H Williams.'*

Chapter 4

ATTENDANCE

Attendance figures loom large in the Logbooks. From the earliest entries in 1863, the average attendances are recorded weekly. Mr. Sayce recorded boys, girls and infants separately, but Mr. Phillip records just the one figure for the Boys' School. The girls are mentioned by him only when boys and girls combine in various activities. By May 1872, attendances were up to over 60 and they continued to rise until the winter set in. The Government grant was based partly on these figures.

There were many reasons for low attendance. Inclement weather – possibly because of the lack of suitable footwear and clothing and the rough access to the school – sickness, including epidemics of measles, smallpox, cholera, 'fevers' (including scarlet fever and typhoid), mumps and whooping cough- and various events in the neighbourhood.

Weather:

On July 23th, 1875, Mr. Phillip recorded:

> *'Closed the schools on Wednesday on account of the very heavy rains swelling out the River so that it was impossible for the children to get to School along the Moors.'*

On October 19th and 20th:

> *'Found it impossible to keep school open as the River is swelled out to such a degree that The Moors is completely submerged from Henley St to the School gate owing to the late rains.'*

We have to remember that School Road did not exist at this time – children had to travel along a lane across the low-lying Moors (the Moor fields) to reach the Schools.

*School Road in the early 1900s. The flooded fields in the
background were behind the school.*

On Oct 27th 1882:

*'As it was utterly impossible for the children to attend school on account of the
unusually high floods on Monday afternoon & Tuesday it was decided to
dismiss the few children & close the school.'* (Boys)

In November:

*'A quantity of snow fell during the night consequently only 31 in attendance this
morning and 57 this afternoon.'* (Infants)

Wet or cold weather affected the youngest children more than the others, and
there are several occasions during the winter of 1885-86 when the Infants'
School had to be closed because there were not enough pupils present to be able,
officially, to mark the registers nor enough to make up a class for teaching:

October 23rd   *'A very wet afternoon only 56 children present, could not mark
               registers.'*

November 3rd *'A very wet morning, had to close school.'*

March 12th   *'The children are still absent owing in great measure to the
               severity of the weather.'*

March 26th   *'The weather still prevents the children attending regularly.'*

This poor weather continued into the spring, and even in May, Miss Clark, Mistress of the Infants' School recorded:

'Obliged to give two days holiday on account of excessive rain, and floods.'

Every winter, similar problems were recorded. For example:

1888   *'The attendance very small owing to the heavy rain, which fell all day.'*
        'Have not been able to send the children to play on the playground all the week owing to wet weather.'
1890   *'Several children under four absent on account of the weather, which is very cold. Today there are very few children at school owing to snow falling.'*
1891   *'The children had no play yesterday afternoon and were dismissed ten minutes earlier on account of a threatened storm.'*
1892   *'The attendance this week is much lower owing to a very heavy fall of snow.'*

In 1893, Miss Clark recorded:

'The average attendance for the week is only 111, owing to the heavy rain showers, and the bad state of the children's boots.'

Then in January 1895:

'Very little slate work taken during the week owing to the extreme cold. Extra marching and collective lessons taken in order to keep the children warm.'

The weather in February 1895 was particularly cold. The attendance was very low, particularly amongst the youngest children and pipes froze so that there was no water supply in the school.

'During the very cold weather the forms and desks are placed as near to the fire as possible.'

Several children stayed away until the end of March when the weather became milder, but this was followed by heavy rainfall, which again reduced the attendance. This had the inevitable consequence:

'The irregular attendance during the winter months has made the class rather weak in all subjects.'

It was not only during the winter that the weather posed problems. In July 1895:

> *'Several children sent home to change their clothes; they having been out in a heavy storm.'*

Then in September:

> *'The classes are taught as much as possible out of doors during the mornings, the sun is too powerful in the afternoons to allow of the playground being used.'*

In June 1896:

> *'Sent the children home at 11.50am as I feared a storm was coming.'*

There was no question of informing parents beforehand of changes in the school day. Children were expected to get themselves to and from school, even the littlest ones with the help of older brothers or sisters or neighbouring children. Parents were, however, expected to inform the school when their children were away, though this was not always done, and there are many cases recorded of teachers checking up on the reasons why individual children were absent. This was done even when there was an Attendance Officer appointed.

Illnesses:

The worst recorded instances of absence due to illness are at the beginning of 1875. On January 29th, Mr. Phillip wrote in the logbook:

> *'Small pox & other epidemic diseases e.g. Scarlet Fever & Whooping Cough have now become so prevalent in the Town that the Schools are almost entirely deserted. Only 5 boys were present on Monday Morning & 14 in the Afternoon. ...The weekly average is 11.9 only... In the 2nd class not one boy attended in a morning.'*

On February 5th, he wrote:

> *'Fresh cases of small pox have again broken out so that the attendance is again most wretched.'*

On February 12th:

> *'Owing to another outbreak of Small pox I have been obliged to send home a few of the boys whose homes are so near those infected as to render it dangerous for them to attend School.'*

There is a slight improvement at the end of that month. On February 26th 1875:

> *'As most of the small pox cases have been removed to the Sanatorium & are going on satisfactorily several other boys have put in an appearance during the week.'*

Numbers did not get back to near normal until the middle of March when the workhouse boys returned to school after an absence of seven weeks. The part-timers did not return immediately as the workshops were still closed.

Two pupils, Alfred Dance and John Laughton, were absent from school for two months in 1876, suffering from Typhoid Fever.

In 1879 there was an outbreak of measles in the Town, which lasted several months:

> *'Sept 19th – A great many children in the Town are laid up with measles.*
> *Nov 14th – Measles still very prevalent in the Town.*
> *Nov 28th – Many of the children returned to school on Monday after being absent for several weeks on account of the measles.'*

In March 1880:

> *'Three medical gentlemen... together with Mr. Gander the Nuisance Inspector* [what we would now call a Health Inspector], *attended the school & examined all the children to see if any are suffering from infectious diseases of any kind the result of which was that several were sent home & are not to be allowed to return without a Medical Certificate.'*

The 'infectious diseases' included ringworm, which was particularly prevalent amongst the inmates of the Workhouse and the poorer areas of the town where people lived in close proximity to one another.

At the end of April 1880:

> *'Still there are many cases of scarlet fever in the Town & many children in consequence are still absent. This scarlet fever has proved a serious hindrance to the children's progress.'*

Miss Carter, the first Mistress of the Infants' School, recorded a scarlet fever outbreak in December 1881, followed by an epidemic of whooping cough. On January 27th 1882 she wrote:

'...a number of children are still absent with the Whooping cough, and others not yet recovered from the fever.'

At the end of February, the attendance was still low, with girls seeming to suffer more than the boys – only 8 out of 20 girls having attended during that week.
    Scarlet fever broke out again in the spring of 1886. On March 5th:

'Many children still absent suffering from bad colds, scarlet fever etc. No less than 31 have been absent the whole of the week.'

In September 1881:

'Mr Fosbrooke the Medical Officer of health visited the school to day & reported that several cases of Diptheria had again broken out in the town, in consequence of which he recommended that F Dyson & all children from Canada [an area between Alcester and the village of Great Alne] *be sent home at once.'*

In the Infants school:

'There are two or three absent with measles & one or two with fever, besides eighteen absent with mumps.'

Even the monitor, Annie Phillip, succumbed and Miss Carter was left in sole charge of between 40 and 50 children.
    In November of the same year:

'owing to a fresh outbreak of the Mumps the attendance has been less even than that of last week.... Found it utterly impossible to make any progress whatever in the school owing to the exceptionally low & irregular attendances.'

On Nov 13th 1882:

'A few children who have been suffering from Mumps during the last fortnight returned to school ... others appeared with bandaged faces and had to be sent home.'

And on November 17th:

> '*No less than 53 children have been absent during this week suffering from the Mumps.*'

In February 1889, there was another epidemic of Measles, with seven families being affected in the first four days. The school was closed completely for five weeks between the beginning of February and the middle of March. This was followed by another outbreak of whooping cough. In the Infants' School:

> '*13 cases of whooping cough reported. The incessant coughing in school renders teaching very difficult.*'

The whooping cough continued, and even in July:

> '*No children with whooping cough are allowed to be at school, but there are many children with bad coughs.*'

In early 1890, there was an outbreak of Russian Influenza: in 1891 it was scarlet fever, mumps and chicken-pox; in 1892, more whooping cough and:

> '*There are 19 cases of sickness, mostly "Mumps" which seem to be increasing rapidly.*' In June, because of this epidemic the school was closed '*for one week by order of Dr. Jephcott.*'

This extended the Summer holiday to five weeks, at the end of which the seemingly annual outbreak of measles occurred.

Measles closed the schools again for five weeks in the spring of 1897.

During the winter of 1900-1901, it was Measles and Whooping Cough which laid low the younger children. In January 1901:

> '*The Object Lessons for this Quarter have been again started, as many of the children are now attending for the first time since the middle of October of last year.*'

Outside Events (See also Chapter 12):

In May 1872, the school was closed early for the visit of Wombwell's Menagerie to Alcester. This Menagerie was a regular visitor to Alcester, as was Fawcett's

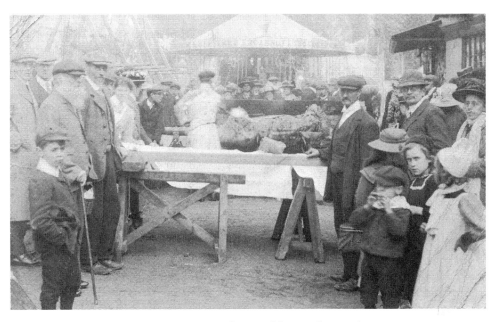

A Mop Fair in Alcester (date unknown).

[Fossett's?] Circus. In August, September and October, poor attendances are recorded because of Redditch Fair, a '*wild beast show*' in Alcester, and Mop fairs '*which are Annually held in Alcester & the neighbouring villages*' as well as an early closure for the annual Sunday School Treat. These occasions gradually became reasons for the Master to award half holidays.

On October 12th 1874 the Master recorded, '*Attendance very poor all day as it is the Statute Fair at Stratford-on-Avon*' and on 13th, '*Attendance very meagre again it being the 2nd Statute Fair day at Alcester*.' This was what we now know as the 'Runaway Mop'.

Cattle Fairs were also occasions for increased absence. On May 28th 1880 attendance was:

> '*somewhat meagre on this day as an important Cattle Sale & Sheep shearing contest were held in the Town.*'

Children also missed school to help with planting and picking potatoes and other horticultural and harvesting work:

In July 9 1875:

> '*Found a great many children absent being employed in the fields & gardens.*'

Warwickshire Imperial Yeomanry in Ragley Park 1905.

In July 1877, Mr. Phillip recorded:

> *'Average attendance much lower this week as many boys have been busy picking fruit whilst others have been absent having gone to view the Worcestershire Volunteers encampment in Ragley Park.'*

In July 1894:

> *'Several children "Babies" absent having gone into the fields with their mothers (pea picking).'*

In October 1881, the Marquis of Hertford was the unwitting cause of *'frightfully low'* attendance when half of the children were:

> *'absent in order to carry home a quantity of firewood which had been sent by the Marquis of Hertford for the benefit of the poor of Alcester. Having however explained to his Lordship's Steward the great injury such an arrangement caused to our Schools, especially at this time of the Year, he promised it should not be given away till 5 pm on all future occasions.'*

It was not only the Boys' school which suffered from children taking time off. In April 1891, Miss Clark in the Infants' school recorded:

> *'Twelve children absent on Thursday afternoon owing to a show being in the town.'*

Attendance had generally improved after the Agricultural Children's Act was brought into effect in January 1876. The original Act of 1873 prohibited the employment of children below the age of eight in agriculture, and tried to ensure minimum school attendance for those aged eight to twelve. However, it was almost entirely ineffective because there was no agency set up to check that the provisions were adhered to.

The 1876 Act required the setting up of school committees to check attendance where there were no school boards. In Alcester the Managers' Committee was empowered to demand compulsory attendance of children in the age range of five to thirteen inclusive. This is the beginning of the appearance of the Attendance Officer or 'Whipper-In'.

There are few mentions by Mr. Phillip of boys specifically playing truant from the Boys' School. The first recorded instance is in early 1876 when George Croft, his brother [probably John] and a boy called Hawtin were kept '*in school without dinner for playing truant.*' This seemed to have little effect on Hawtin, as he again played truant the following day. Some of the Croft children from Bleachfield Street seem to have been particularly difficult. In August 1887 Charles Croft, a younger brother of George and John is also mentioned for playing truant. Then in September, '*Charles Croft brought to school by his elder brother at a quarter to eleven, having been found loitering in the fields.*'

The next mention is in February 1878 when Mr. Phillip '*kept Tom Eddin in school during dinner hour on Tuesday & Thursday according to his parents' request for playing truant*' a rare early instance of home-school cooperation. Another occurred in 1885 when Mr. Phillip '*Punished Ernest Pritchard at his mother's request for playing truant yesterday afternoon.*'

In November 1878, Mr. Phillip wrote:

'*Gave no Scripture Lesson on Thursday morning as the room was wanted for a short time for a Public Meeting at which Bye Laws were agreed upon for the sanction of the School Attendance Committee.*'

The Attendance Bye Laws were suspended for a month in the autumn of 1879 because of an outbreak of measles in the Town, but in May 1880 is recorded:

'*Punished three boys for playing truant yesterday morning.*'

In 1882, the Bye Laws were again suspended from August until the end of September, which had an effect on the attendance:

> '*Sepr 8th   Attendance very meagre indeed Avg. only 80.2. This irregular attendance is no doubt caused by the suspension of the Bye-Laws wh: suspension will extend to Sepr. the 25th.*'

and on the education of the children:

> '*Sepr 29th Several more children again returned to school on Monday morning in a very backward state.*'
> '*Oct 6th   The wretchedly poor attendances made by many of the 1st class boys will at once account for such backwardness.*'

In November 1880, the School was asked to intervene to help a parent when:

> '*at the urgent & special request of Alb Malins Church St his son Herbert was somewhat severely punished for playing truant & constantly spending his school fees no less than 1/3 [6½p] being thus unaccounted for.*'

There is no record of what the severe punishment was, nor that for John Bayliss of Meeting Lane who:

> '*was somewhat severely punished for constantly playing truant notwithstanding all the warnings he has received. This case was aggravated by his persistent lying & his obstinate & wilful disobedience in even the simplest matters.*'

In the Infants department, Miss Carter recorded punishing:

> '*a child for playing truant by keeping him after the others had been dismissed.*'

Rarely, it was necessary to suspend, or even to expel boys, but there seems to have been a spate of expulsions at the end of 1880. On Dec. 7th 1880, Mr. Phillip '*Expelled C Hopkins from the school for wilful & systematic disobedience & also for a gross insult on the master & his Senior Pupil Teacher.*' On the following day, he '*Consented to re-admit C Hopkins on condition that he renders a humble apology & undergoes corporal punishment to be inflicted by the master with the written consent of his father.*'

> On Dec 14th '*Expelled Alfred Houghton from school for wilful disobedience, rudeness & impertinence.*'
> and on 16th '*Expelled John Steele, Jno Croft & Fr Dyson from school for obstinate, wilful & deliberate disobedience & impertinence. Also sent Alfred Houghton back home until he is willing to comply with my request.*'

On the following day is recorded:

'Consented to re-admit John Steele, Jno Croft & Fr Dyson on condition that they render a humble apology, promise that such conduct shall not be repeated and undergo corporal punishment to be inflicted by the master with the written consent of the parent.

F Dyson, one of the parents, expressed a desire to remain & witness the punishment & on doing so declared himself perfectly satisfied & promised for the future to leave his boy entirely in the master's hands.'

In 1885, three boys were suspended from the school – two Bayliss boys forcibly removed by their mother and refused re-admission until an apology was received – and the other for a physical attack on the Master. The former case was taken up by solicitors and the Government's Education Department. More details of this are given in Chapter 9.

The Attendance Officer, Mr. Cook, visited the school in July 1882 after Mr. Phillip had recorded:

'Found the attendances falling off throughout the school as many children are engaged in making hay & picking fruit,' and *'Children extensively employed in picking fruit this week.'*

Attendances became so irregular in June 1884 that the Attendance Officer decided to summons two of the worst families in the Magistrate's Court *'as a warning to the others'*. Despite this, attendance was down again because of the pea-picking season. It must have been difficult for poor families to decide whether or not to risk a summons by keeping their children at home to help in seasonal work. Most could not afford to miss out on the extra money which could be earned by their children in this way.

Numbers of children registered at the schools could change daily because there were no standardised entry and leaving dates. There are constant references, both in the Boys' and Infants' Schools of children being admitted mid-term or even mid-week. They also left at any time, and there seems also to be a transient community which moved from place to place to find work and children were moved in and out of the schools. In October 1890, Miss Clark recorded:

'Three children have left the school, their parents having gone away from the town. Seven have left from the first class during the year from the same cause.'

Pea Picking.

Allwood's Needle Factory, Minerva Mill, c. 1900.

The maximum school leaving age at this time was 13. Boys usually went to work in one of the local needle workshops or factories, or to work on the land as an agricultural labourer. Occasionally a boy might be apprenticed to a trader, often within the family. The main workshop/factory owners in Alcester were Dowdeswell, Allwood, Haywood, Skinner – all involved in the making of needles – and Averill, a twine manufacturer.

Girls usually went into 'service', occasionally some distance from home. It was quite usual for middle class families and single people to have servants. Sometimes boys or girls left the school at an earlier age to go to work, only to return some time later when they were no longer required, so long as they were still under 13.

In April 1880, an inspection was carried out by the local Factories Inspector and a senior Schools Inspector from London. They found two boys being employed full-time illegally. Charles Strain and John Hemming were ordered to return to school.

Sometimes the punishment for non-attendance seems odd. On July 16th 1880, Mr. Phillip:

'sent F Bleaney home on Thursday Morning as his mother fetched him from School last night without first obtaining permission to do so.'

On 23rd, he wrote:

'F Bleaney appeared in School again on Monday but was again sent home to ask for a satisfactory explanation from his mother.'

In March 1881 we see the first reference to the Attendance Officer, when the Master sent him a report because of the low numbers in the 4th class. This obviously had an effect as:

'Several boys in the 4th class returned to school on Monday Morning owing to the interference of the Attendance officer.'

The Attendance Bye-Laws were once again suspended from August to early September 1881 and 1882. In September 1882, Miss Carter recorded:

'The attendance this week has been rather low probably on account of the Bye-laws being suspended for three weeks on account of the Harvest.'

The children took full advantage of this suspension, whether or not they were involved in the harvesting.

Occasionally it was necessary for Mr. Phillip himself to be absent from school:

Sept 22nd 1875	*'Master absent all day having gone to the Festival of the Three Choirs held at Worcester.'*
Nov 22nd 1875	*'Master absent a short time in the afternoon being busy preparing for an Entertainment to be given in the evening.'*
July 3rd 1877	*'Absent the whole of this day having to attend the Quarter Sessions at Warwick as a witness in a case of Felony.'*
April 1st 1881	*'Master absent during a portion of the afternoon in order to attend a Confirmation Service in St Nicholas' Church Alcester.'*

Mr. Phillip seems to have been waging a constant struggle to educate boys who knew little when they first started school and were unwilling to learn. There was little parental support, and school hours and days were regularly interrupted by holidays, foul weather and the draw of regular Statute Fairs, cattle sales, 'treats' and health epidemics. However, the numbers of children at the school kept increasing, until that in itself became a problem.

In 1880 Mr. Phillip experienced:

'great difficulty in attempting to carry out the Time Table as the Desk accommodation is totally inadequate for the number of children now attending the school.'

There was some encouragement to reduce absenteeism, which was still somewhat of a problem, so on the afternoon of Friday 5th November 1886, Mr. William Gardner, the new Master, decided that:

'those children who have made 10 attendances during the past week were allowed to leave school at 4.15.'

Further attempts were made by the Managers in 1887 when they:

'promised a return of one half-penny to all who have made the full attendances for each week, the total sum to be repaid at the end of each quarter in school fees & books.'

This did have some effect, for Mr. Gardner recorded on February 11th:

'Good progress has been made this week. All the standards are improving in their work. This is probably due to a better attendance.'

During the week ending 6th May 1887:

'85 boys have made from eight to twelve full attendances during the past quarter.'

William Gardner was not impressed by the Attendance Officer. In July 1887, following a decline in attendance because of the pea picking, he wrote:

'Mr Cook, Attendance Officer, seldom or never visits the school. He sent the register to-day for the first time in six weeks.'

There were several cases when Mr. Gardner tried to ascertain the reason for absence himself. In August 1887, he wrote:

'I sent to enquire the cause of absence of A. Mews, and ascertained that the family have left the town.'

He even went so far as to visit the Union workhouse to discover:

'that the two Houghtons & Wm. Newman have left the "House".'

No-one had thought to inform the school. In March 1888, he recorded:

'Several lads are away this week on paltry excuses... Sending names to the Attendance Officer has no apparent effect.'

Attendance continued to worsen during that spring, despite Mr. Gardner's own efforts to chase up the boys, and the poor academic performance of those irregular attendees were noted. During the last week of April:

'Sixteen boys have been absent the whole of the week.'

At the end of April, Mr. Milman, Her Majesty's Inspector (H.M.I.), paid an unannounced visit to the school and was:

'sorry there is reason for complaint about the attendance.'

During one week in May, 20% of the boys had been absent.

A notable absentee was Henry Salmon, who was recorded as a persistent truant from April 1888. In October:

'Harry Salmon's mother and grandmother are continually coming to the school with the information that he is playing truant. He is utterly beyond the control of his friends.'

The Davis brothers, George and Harry, were constantly playing truant throughout 1890 and 1891, despite the fact that their father had been taken to court and fined. It was not unusual for them to absent themselves from school for several weeks at a time. In June 1891, Mr. Cook, the Attendance Officer, had promised to call into the school to discuss the problem, but on 12th June, Mr. Gardner recorded:

'The week has gone, but the Attendance Officer did not put in an appearance.'

Miss Clark, too, had little time for the Attendance Officer. As late as 1897, she wrote:

'Sent a short Absentee List to Mr. Cook (Attendance Officer) who rarely calls to ascertain what children are absent.'

In December 1898, she sent her Assistant to check on the absent children:

'Miss Cooper went after all absentees on Monday morning. Illness was given as the reason of absence in all cases but one.'

The Attendance Officer called at the school two days later.
  Mr. Cook was replaced in 1899 by Mr. Boddington, who seems to have been a more regular visitor to the school, but Miss Clark still found it necessary to enlist her Assistant's help:

'Jan 8th   Re-opened school. 80 children present.
*   12   Miss Cooper visited absentees and on Tuesday morning 90 were present.'*

In the 1890 Infant logbook, there is mention of a scheme of Attendance tickets, where children were awarded points for each time they attended school, these points being taken away for every absence – including on account of illness. In 1892, Miss Clark reported:

'The children seem to take an interest in gaining the Attendance Tickets, and try to come to school in good time.'

In November, the children received prizes in return for their tickets.

> *'The children had "songs" and "recitations" instead of the usual lessons. The Rector and several visitors being present besides the children's parents. Three children gained "Medals" having gained the full number of marks.'*

This scheme seemed to have had an effect on many children, though not all. In March 1893, Miss Clark wrote:

> *'Twelve children absent on account of a Circus being in the town.'*

On May 5th:

> *'Six children have lost their Attendance Tickets this week through staying away from school, and two from illness,'* but on May 12th, *'Twenty three children have not been absent from school at all during the past three months, and eleven have not been absent during the present school year.'*

In December 1894, instead of medals for full attendance:

> *'the "Prizes" for regular attendance (consisting chiefly of articles of warm clothing) were distributed.'*

It is evident that the improvements in the boys' education was achieved through the hard work of Mr. Phillip, with the support of the Managers – in particular the Rev. Alfred H. Williams – and Lord Hertford. A pity, then, that his reputation is tarnished in later years (Chapter 10).

We do not have the logbooks for the Girls' School, but the Minute books record the Managers' approval of the work done by Mrs. Fanny Bates.

Chapter 5

SETBACKS

As a result of irregular attendance, many boys were reported as being 'very backward' in reading and other school subjects. Mr. Phillip did try to help these boys by giving extra time to the basic work. He seems determined to raise the standards in the school. On Examination in July 1881 he found that:

> *'Several are still very backward and will, for some time, require special care.'* In September, *'Finding the 1st Standard boys much behind in their work both I & my assistant spent a great portion of our time with them.'*

Despite the prevalence of epidemics being *'a hindrance'*, the end of 1880 seems to have been a watershed for the school. There were far more children attending classes, and more boys achieving success in the standard assessment tests and the extra subjects, as well as winning scholarships to the Grammar School. Her Majesty's Inspector commented favourably on the discipline and efficiency of the Master, and he had the support of parents. The H.M.I. did, however, recommend that:

> *'The Boys School would benefit by the formation of a distinct Infant Department as the little Boys would come up into the first standard better prepared,'* and that a second Pupil Teacher be employed.

The Infants' Department was set up with three classes after the summer holiday in 1881. It was placed in the temporary charge of Miss Mary A. Carter, a certified teacher, with Edith Jackson as an unqualified assistant. There were 68 children on the books on the first day. This quickly rose to 88, but by March 1882, the average attendance had regularly fallen to below 50, and Miss Jackson had to leave:

> *'as Teacher in the school; the numbers being too low for her services to be required at present.'*

Miss Carter was not happy about this and wrote:

'Have had no one to help me this week so was obliged to take all the children myself, which is rather a drawback as each class is obliged to be left more or less to itself during the day, especially in the writing lessons.'

In May 1882, the Diocesan Inspector's Report was received:

'from which it appears that 52 per cent [of the children] *were ranked as excellent & 98 per cent passed. Out of the 9 different subjects 7 were marked "Excellent", 1 Good & 1 Fair.'*

In June 1882, Mr. Phillip wrote:

'Examined the 1st Standard boys in Reading again. Found a slight improvement though many of them are still very backward. Also examined the upper standards in Arithmetic. Found that some of the boys in St IV will still require an unlimited amount of patience & perseverance.'

He believed that much of the problem stemmed from the poor teaching in the Infants' department, so that the boys had few skills when they came into the Boys' School. In the new Infants' School, Miss Carter had her own problems with the children. Also in June 1882, she wrote:

'Examined First class Reading again this week, & find the same children backward: this can be accounted for by their irregular attendance especially the girls, one making 4 attendances and another 6 during the week.'

Her Majesty's Inspector was also greatly concerned over the Infants' attendance. In his Report for 1882, he wrote:

'The attendance is most unsatisfactory. Out of 106 Children whose names are on the books, 36 only have made sufficient attendance to be examined..... Such irregularity not only makes efficiency in the Infant School impossible, but it already very seriously injures the prospects of both the upper Departments, and threatens ... to do still more. The matter calls for immediate action on the part of the Managers.'

It must be remembered that Miss Carter was the only teacher in the Infants' School, with an inexperienced monitor, trying to teach up to 80 children from the age of 3 to 6 years in one room. In April 1883, when the numbers passed 90, she was *'Obliged to engage an additional monitor ... to take the younger children.'* During one day of that month, there were 100 children in attendance.

One of Mr. Phillip's daughters, Annie, was taken on as an extra monitor, which did ease the situation a little, though numbers continued to rise. By September 1883, the numbers had increased to over 100 with Miss Carter being the only teacher, assisted by two monitors – Annie Phillip and Annie Cull. In November, she wrote:

> *'Attendance about as usual, had 116 present on Monday afternoon but the number have only reached 110 the remainder of the week.'*

Despite all the extra work he put in, sometimes Mr. Phillip had to admit:

> *'several boys showed themselves to be very backward; in fact almost hopeless.'*

However, after more work with these boys:

> *'at the end of the week a decided improvement was noticeable.'*

In 1882, there was some co-operation with the Attendance Officer and the Factories Inspector to try to cut down on the absences which hindered the progress of the children in the school:

> *'Decr. 8th – Mr. Cook the Attendance Officer paid a visit to the school & inspected the Registers. With a view to securing more regularity in the attendance I promised to make out a list of absences weekly.'*

To further help the 'backward' boys, Mr. Phillip made temporary reorganisations of the classes, on occasions subdividing them into smaller groups, especially for Reading, or providing extra support:

> May 4th 1883   *'Examined the boys in Standard I & found many so very backward that it was necessary to supply that class with two Teachers.'*

Commercially produced learning materials were becoming more available, and the Master seemed keen to make use of these. At the upper end of the school, boys were using text books for Geography, namely Nelson's Geographical Readers, and in 1883 new Historical Readers were introduced. Also in 1883 Arithmetic Cards were introduced to the Standard III boys.

The larger numbers of children and the increased amount of written work threw up another problem – the lack of space. In March 1885:

'Attendance is the highest during the last 3 months [135.6]. Schoolroom very full. Experienced great difficulty in Dictation & Writing Lessons in consequence.'

Families were required to pay for their children's Copy Books, but it was sometimes difficult to collect the money. On June 8th 1883, Mr. Phillip *'Sent several boys back for Copy Book money.'* He was still trying to collect this money up to the beginning of the Harvest Holidays in August. In October, he sent two boys home *'until their parents would supply them with 2d for a copy book.'* In November he sent two Ellins brothers *'home till their parents consented to purchase copy books for them. Both returned on the following day with the money.'*

There were still problems with incoming children at the lower end of the school, and this was recognised in H.M.I.'s Report for 1884:

'This school [the Boys' School] has suffered from a sudden influx of backward children fifteen of whom had never been to school till the last sixteen months. Consequently many of the boys in the first Standard are hopelessly behind but the rest have been well taught & the school has passed generally well.'

Mary Carter's term of engagement came to an end on December 21st 1883. She was replaced by Miss Mary Clark at the beginning of 1884.

The numbers attending the schools continued to increase, bringing the problem of overcrowding and the difficulties of trying to teach a large number of children of different abilities in the same classroom. There was also the continuing problem of boys not doing "Home Lessons". In May 1884 the number of boys on the School Books was 140, and the Assistant Teacher, George Herbert Smith, resigned to go to America.

By the beginning of October, Mr. Phillip was feeling the strain. Several advertisements had been placed in the 'Schoolmaster' newspaper, but there had been no applications for the post of Assistant Master. At the end of the month he:

'Received valuable assistance this week from Mr. Withers, Assistant Master, Astwood Bank their school being shut up on account of Measles.'

Mr. Withers was able to stay until the middle of November, and proved to be very useful.

In November 1884, 128 boys were presented for examination by Her Majesty's Inspector, though nine of these were excused the examination because of sickness or 'dullness'. 85 per cent of the boys passed the examination – a remarkable result considering the staffing difficulties that Mr. Phillip had encountered during the year. Out of the 119 boys presented for the Writing examination only 4 failed.

By November 1885, with 171 boys on the books, the school was:

'full to overflowing' and Mr. Phillip *'experienced very great difficulties not only from lack of space & desk accommodation but also from lack of staff.'* He *'Re-organised the school & found it necessary to make 5 classes instead of 4 as heretofore thus another difficulty arises in trying to carry on the work of the School.'*

The end-of-year Inspectors' Report for 1885 reflected the problems faced by the overcrowded, understaffed school:

'I am sorry to find a great falling off in the quality of the work and the Discipline of the school is not exact enough especially in the lower standards. On these grounds I have great hesitation in recommending any Merit Grant. Spelling is bad and Arithmetic weak. Grammar too is insufficiently known.'

During the year, four Assistant Teachers had come and gone in the Boys' School – Mr. Dodson, Mr. Lloyd, Mr. Selvage and Mr. Beattie. Discipline seems to have broken down somewhat, and many more boys were being kept in after school hours for late attendance and not doing home work.

In the Infants' School, too, the Inspectors found problems:

'This school has not improved... and shows no advance on last year. The Children too are fidgety and not very attentive... I do not mean to say that the school is inefficient, but it is not so strong as I expected to find it.'

At the end of November 1885, the Managers gave permission for three boys – George Davis, A. Goodison and Leonard King – to be sent back to the Infant school after entering the Boys' school at the beginning of the month *'as they do not yet know their letters.'* However, the Inspectors made it very clear that:

'Children over seven years of age should not be kept here [the Infants' School] *except by the express authority of the managers.'*

Mr. Phillip, Mrs Bates, Miss Carter and Miss Clark had done their best, but the schools in 1886 had many problems, including lack of space, inadequate ventilation, too few desks, a shortage of trained teaching staff, difficulties getting children to do home work and getting parents to provide exercise books and paying the school fees.

Chapter 6

A NEW BEGINNING

On August 16th 1886, after the Harvest Holiday, the handwriting in the logbook suddenly changes as the Managers found it necessary to replace Mr. John Phillip with Mr. William Gardner. (See Chapter 10)

Mr. Gardner's impressions of the school were not good. His first entries read:

'Opened school at 9 a.m. Found the children very fidgety and disobedient. They pay little or no heed to orders, and are very careless in all they do... About three fourths of the boys are without exercise books in the Upper Standards... The arithmetic is shockingly bad... St IV know nothing at all about Grammar. The majority of them cannot pick out simple nouns and verbs.'

He took stock of the resources available, and the abilities of each standard and found both wanting. Mr. Gardner was determined to impose discipline and make changes. It is obvious that he would stand no nonsense. On September 3rd he wrote:

'Several children have been caned for coming late. Most of the children have paid for Copy Books & Exercises,' and on September 13th, *'Sent about half-a-dozen boys home for school fees. Cautioned the children about climbing the walls & trees.'*

On November 8th 1886:

'The boys are very talkative to-day. Obtained order after using the cane on the worst of the delinquents.'

On December 17th:

'The two Jobsons and two Westburys have been sent home this week having failed to bring school fees.'

Mr. Gardner had no qualms about using the cane when other methods had been tried and failed. For example, on May 10th 1887, he:

'Punished, with the cane, the careless boys in St. II & IV for the bad spelling they did in the Dictation Exercise, warnings and writing punishments having proved of no avail.'

In June:

'William Ellins was punished three times for repeated disobedience to his teacher, 1st with one stroke on the hand, 2nd with one, 3rd with two.'

More punishments were recorded, but not all parents approved of the hard line taken, and some took their children away from the school:

'March 25th   George Skinner had frequently to be punished for bad behaviour and indifference in his work.

May 20th   Sent to enquire the cause of absence of George Skinner; the messenger was told that he has gone to Coughton School.'

The H.M.I. Report in December 1886 recognised the previous difficulties at the school and the improvements made by Mr. Gardner. It also insisted that further changes were made, otherwise Government Grants would be lost:

'Although the attainments of the Boys are, naturally enough, hardly up to the average at present, much good work has been done, and there is every promise of efficiency. I am particularly pleased with the improved tone of the school.

The staff of the Boys' School should be at once strengthened so as to meet the requirements of Art. 83, which are not at present satisfied.'

In December 1886, Mr. Gardner *'Sent an advertisement to the "Schoolmaster" at the Rector's request, in order to obtain an Assistant and a Transfer P.T. in 2nd or 3rd Year.'* The "Schoolmaster" was a magazine for teaching professionals, in which there were also job advertisements. The School was obviously looking for a qualified teacher and an experienced Pupil Teacher with two or three years to complete of his apprenticeship.

Although Henry Singleton was appointed to start work in January 1887, there were no applications from Pupil Teachers. Fred Whiting and later Albert Tompkins were appointed as paid Monitors to help the teachers.

It was not until after Henry left in December 1887 to go to Caernarvon Teacher Training College, that two further Assistant Masters were appointed – Joe Downing Breffit and Charles Thornton Howes. Both eighteen-year-olds had successfully completed their Pupil Teacher apprenticeships. Mr. Breffit came from Somercotes National School, Derbyshire, and Mr. Howes from Holme Board School in West Yorkshire. Like Alcester, Holme School had benefitted from Earnshaw's Charity (See Chapter 7).

In the Infants' School, the Mistress, Mary Clark, and her new Assistant, Mary Cooper, were working hard to improve the education of the children and despite the continued references to irregular attendances, the HMI's 1887 Report read:

'The Infants have made marked progress. Their work is done smartly and in good style, and the answering lively and general.'

In the Boys' School, the hard work done by Mr. Gardner and his young Assistants produced, in 1888, the best report yet – despite the attendance problems:

'The boys are in good order and have made thoroughly good progress during the year. Reading is accurate ... and the boys answer well on the meanings. Writing is of a good style ... and Spelling is well done throughout ... Arithmetic is well done as also is the English. Geography has been added with some success, though not very interesting at present. The boys sing well.'

In 1889:

'Five boys named Arthur Andrews, Harry Fryer, William Cook, John Jackson and Alfred Blackband have been elected free scholar in the Abbey Grammar School.'

This was the largest number to gain scholarships in any one year.

You can almost feel Mr. Gardner's pleasure in the progress of his pupils, for example in his logbook entry for July 10th 1889:

'St. I has improved wonderfully the last month. About half-a-dozen were very deficient on issuing from the Infants School, but they have begun to move at last.'

And again in January 1890:

'The order is much better this week, & the boys seem to have got into a proper swing with their work.'

Achievements must have improved as the incidence of boys being 'very backward' are rare enough for those boys to be individually identifiable – e.g. in December 1889 are mentioned Frank Stevens, Charles Haywood and Victor

Styler. Styler is later mentioned as an irregular attendee, together with John Smith, Frank Arnall, George Emms and Andrew Wright.

But you can also feel Mr. Gardner's frustration when recording, also in July 1889:

> *'Punished three boys for playing truant all day yesterday. This offence seems to be on the increase.'*

and in February 1890:

> *'The absence of so many in the school proves a great obstacle to satisfactory progress.'*

There is also a tone of discontent when he recorded some of the many half- and full-day holidays which had become *'usual'* following school Inspections, and days off for Treats.

In May 1890 he wrote:

> *'Following the precedent of other years, holiday was given this afternoon in honour of the Bishop's visit to hold a Confirmation.'*

(See also Chapter 12)

Although Mr. Gardner had become frustrated with the breaks in the boys' education, the Alcester schools seemed to do better than some others locally. In the Infants' logbook for 1891 is recorded:

> *'March 2nd*   *Have this day entered a girl Elizth. Payne over six years of age, who does not know her letters. She has been attending the Roman Catholic School for some time.*
>
> *April 27. 91*   *Have this day entered a boy named Clarence Verney S. Hodgman five years old in 1890 (June) who has been very little to school, he cannot write, and only knows a few of his letters, the parents only came to the town a week ago.'*

In February 1892:

> *'A Pupil Teacher from the Arrow School has been present during the Varied Occupation Lessons for the past three weeks on Wednesday afternoons.'*

No doubt this was so that the apprentice could pick up ideas and gain experience from a larger school.

During the spring of the following year, more children were admitted into the Infants' School, whose education had been neglected, either by having attended a 'dame school' or no school at all. In March, Miss Clark:

'Admitted a girl (at the request of the Girls' Mistress) who will be eight years old in July....she scarcely knows her letters, and cannot write.'

A few days later:

'Another girl over 6 years of age admitted, at the mother's request, she is very backward in most subjects.'

In April:

'Thirteen children have been admitted this week, including a child (Eleanor Shrimpton) who will be six in August who has not been to school before.'

[Note: This same Eleanor Shrimpton became a monitress in the Infants' School in 1901, but was considered not to be a *'suitable teacher for babies, she would do better in a school for older children.'*]

The numbers in the Infants' School increased to the extent that in July 1894 Miss Clark was instructed to advertise for another Assistant Mistress. Unfortunately, this proved rather difficult, and in October:

'Three advertisements were answered during the last fortnight, but still we are not successful in getting another assistant.'

This was recognised in the H.M.I. Report at the end of the year:

'The highest variable Grant is again recommended in consideration of many good features in the conduct of the school, but it is now evident that additional help is required to enable Miss Clark to maintain this department in a thoroughly efficient state. The Infants' School accommodation is at present insufficient for the average attendance. This should be at once remedied or the Grant next year will be endangered.'

It was not until February 1895 that Miss Lily Cook, an ex-pupil teacher from Great Alne Mixed School was appointed as an Assistant Teacher. She stayed only a few months and was followed in quick succession by Miss Wood then Miss A. M. Gray, who stayed until the end of the school year 1899.

Progress was certainly being made in the Infants' School, and was noted by the Government Inspector, though there were occasions when the whole department had to be re-arranged to suit the number in each age group. For example, in May 1896:

> *'The "Babies" are getting too large a class for one Teacher to manage satisfactorily. Those children who have made attendances since November really require more attention than can be given to them as part of the whole class.'*

It is obvious that Miss Clark, Miss Cooper and Miss Gray worked well together, and Miss Clark concerned herself with her Assistants' wellbeing. During the same month as she recorded the overlarge "Baby" class, she notes:

> *'Miss Gray needs help in the Baby Room – the continual strain of talking is telling on her voice and general health.'*

In June:

> *'Miss Gray is so far from well that she cannot manage the whole of the third class in the afternoon... A monitor is greatly needed to enable the classes to work successfully... Miss Gray has not been able to take any oral lessons during the week, but has helped with the other work although far from well.'*

Finally, in July:

> *'Have had to engage a monitress to help in the Baby Room.'*

Sore throats and laryngitis are still experienced by newly qualified teachers, especially those in Infant Schools, who have to use their voices almost non-stop during the school day.

At the end of the Boys' School logbook, there is an entry by Mr. Sayce, made in 1865, which illustrates the difference between the teaching at his time and the achievements of Mr. Phillip and Mr. Gardner. The entry is a list of targets to be reached by the boys in each year group. As well as basic Arithmetic and Reading, they were expected to have learned:

'at the end of

the	2nd year	50 lines of poetry
	III year	40 lines of prose
	IV year	100 lines of poetry with those previously repeated
	V year	80 lines of prose with the 40 lines before learned.'

Compare this with the expectations of the Examiners in the 1890s; Reading (with expression and understanding), Arithmetic, Mental Arithmetic, Writing, Dictation (including Spelling), Poetry, Recitation, History, Geography, Scripture, Drawing, Sewing and Knitting, Singing and Drill [Physical exercises].

However, the level of achievement is much below what is expected today. Miss Clark records with pride that:

'The second class [aged approx. 5-6 years] *have passed a very creditable examination in all subjects. The Reading and Slate work being particularly good. Mental Arithmetic (easy addition up to 10) being well done in most cases.... The third class* [approx. 4-5 years] *has greatly improved.... Words of two and three letters were fairly well known.'*

Both Teachers and Managers must have been pleased to receive the Inspector's report for 1896:

'No pains are spared by Miss Clark and her Assistants to make this a good Infants' School, and the children seem very happy in their work.'

The Infants were making such good progress, that in October 1897:

'A set of Reading Books from the Boys' school has been in use during the week.'

From the beginning of 1898, a new phenomenon entered the Schools – the Record Book:

'Feb. 2nd	*Examined all the children in the school* [Infants] *and entered the results in the "Record Books".*
April 6th	*Class III were examined on Tuesday and the results entered in the Record Book.'*

Teachers in the Infants School – and probably the Boys' and Girls' Schools – were required to examine the children on a regular basis and enter the test results in these new Record Books. It provided a broader basis for the H.M.I. to judge the progress of the children in the schools.

Standards in the Infants' School continued to rise and the Government Inspector reported at the end of 1898:

> *'There is always much to be pleased with in this Infants' School. The teachers work hard and successfully.'*

At the end of 1899, there was even more praise for the school:

> *'There is the same earnestness of purpose in the conduct of this school. The children are bright and receptive, and the attainments in elementary subjects are in advance of the ordinary infants' school requirements.'*

But the Inspector also noted:

> *'The staff of the Infants' School should be at once strengthened so as to meet the requirements of Art 73. of the Code.'*

Miss Gray, who had previously left, was brought back temporarily when the newly-appointed assistant failed to take up the position, and the two monitresses were asked to stay. Miss Gray stayed a month, but had another post to go to. However, in April:

> *'The assistant appointed having asked to be released, Miss Gray returns to this school as soon as possible.'*

Alice Shrimpton, one of the Monitresses was released, but in May the school was still short-staffed and:

> *'It is impossible to follow the Time Table always without another Assistant, as Classes I & II must often be taken together.'*

Alice returned to the school until the end of the month, when it was hoped that Miss Gray would leave her post and return to Alcester. Miss Gray was released to help out at the school for two days during the absence of the Mistress, and there was great relief when she returned as a full-time Assistant on June 11th.

On June 15th Miss Clark wrote:

'This is the first week since March 16th in which the work has been carried on without interruption. The Baby Room will require great attention in consequence of the continual change of Teachers.'

Miss Gray did make a difference, since on 21st June:

'The discipline in the Baby Room has greatly improved during the past two weeks.'

However, at the end of the year the Inspector reported:

'This school continues to be conducted in a very efficient manner, but the unsettled state of the staff has somewhat affected the attainments.'

There was also criticism in 1902 when an unannounced visit by the Inspector, Mr. Tomaline, found that, although Miss Gray was qualified to teach up to 30 children, she had 63 in her class on that particular day. Fortunately it was only a couple of weeks before the end of the school year when many of the "Babies" were moved up into the next class.

At the end of that year, before the school was taken over by Warwickshire County Council, Miss Clark wrote:

'The work has made steady progress since the Commencement of the school year.'

Infants' Class 1908.

Chapter 7

THE BUILDINGS

Prominent Victorians tended to be generous in setting up Charity funds to help the disadvantaged. In Alcester, in addition to the perhaps, better-known Newport and Smallwood charities, Brandis' and Earnshaw's were two charitable trusts set up to help pay for apprenticeships for poor boys. Because the boys originally intended to benefit from these charities were obliged to attend school under the 1870 Education Act, it was felt that access to the funds – some £350 (approx. £16,000 at today's values) – would be very useful towards the cost of the new Schools. Legal advice was taken and the matter referred to the Charity Commissioners.

When the new regime of schooling began, it was recommended by the Marquis of Hertford that fees be raised and a new scale of charges was produced. Children paid according to how many days they attended, and reductions were made for multiple children from the same family in the same department i.e. two or more girls, boys or infants.

Another problem raised its head early in 1872 – the artesian well in the School grounds was found to be contaminated and the water unfit to drink. (The school was situated next door to the cemetery!) In view of this, and the inconvenience of the approach to the Schools, it was suggested that a completely new school be built on a more elevated site. The Marquis of Hertford offered another possible plot of land but warned that the cost of building a new school could be as much as £2000 (£91,500 at today's values).

It was decided to enlarge the existing site, and the transfer of extra land was made in October 1872, though the Trustees had to sign:

'a promise to reconvey the land to Lord Hertford in the event of the Schools not being carried out on the Voluntary principle.' [i.e. under the control of the Church].

After several changes, Mr. G. Hunt, Architect, finally produced plans to include two School Houses and accommodation for 300 children. These were sent to the local Council – at that time Alcester Rural District Council – and the Education Department in London. They were finally approved in January 1873.

In June of that year, tenders for the reconstruction of the Schools were considered and that of Mr. William Hunt of Alcester being the lowest (£1450), it was accepted. He did add that should the price of building materials fall during the construction, he would adjust his bill! Building works began during the summer of 1873, the Boys' and Girls' Schools being temporarily housed in the Town Hall.

This was not really suitable for the large number of children involved, and the Schools had to be closed on days when the Town Hall was required by other organisations. Mr. Phillip reports in October 1883:

'Still at the Town Hall. There being only 6 desks for all the children very few could write in Copy Books. Found the room very close & children noisy.'

In the meantime, the Managers had been trying to raise the money to pay for the Schools.

In April 1872:

'It was resolved that the parish should be canvassed for contributions towards defraying the cost of building the new Schools & in the following order:

District No 1. Commencing in the Priory Street and including the left or north side of the Town extending to Gunnings Bridge taken by Mr Grizzell & Mr J Williams
District 2. Taking Evesham Street and the opposite side to No 1. And terminating at Gunnings Bridge – Messrs T Averill & W Allwood
District 3. Outlying Including Farmers and holders of property not residing in either district Mr A Jackson & Mr B Hughes.'

It was also:

'Proposed by Mr Wyman that steps be taken immediately to ascertain if the surplus money now in the hands of the Bailiffs and Churchwardens can be appropriated in aid of the Schools.'

The canvass of parishioners raised a promised total of £464, which was reported in the Alcester Chronicle. When the time came to call in the promises, some townspeople and, in particular, the local farmers proved very slow in paying over the money.

The Managers were promised a building grant of £348.15.7 [£348.80] from the Education Department:

'not obtainable until the whole amount due on the buildings is paid less the above named sum.'

The Charity Commissioners agreed to the diversion of Brandis and Earnshaw Charity money (£180 and £165 respectively), but a meeting in April 1874 showed the building fund account in deficit by over £239.

The progress of the building work was also a problem. In October 1873 the Managers expressed their disappointment at the progress, and in June 1874 they were still not completed. In August:

'The Secretary was desired to write to Mr George Hunt and request him to come and inspect the Buildings and point out what work was yet required to be done in order to facilitate their completion.'

It was not until September 1874 that the Architect's Certificate of the completion of the building was received, together with bills from the building contractor. It was decided to borrow money from the Stourbridge and Kidderminster Bank to pay off the building account and so secure the Government Grant.

It was decided that the parishioners should be asked for more donations and an advertisement placed in the Alcester Chronicle. The Managers were still trying to pay off the loan in 1877 when odd works in Mrs. Bates' house were being completed. Another trawl of parishioners was made, and school fees raised again.

The water from the Artesian well in the School grounds was very hard and not suitable for drinking, so in July 1877 rainwater downpipes were altered so that they fed cisterns with soft water for school use, but a few months later, perhaps because of dry weather, the Headmaster was instructed to:

'purchase water for the Schools and School houses at the rate of a pail for each.'

The well water did not go to waste. In 1879 the Sanitary Authority wrote *'requiring the existing School drains to be diverted and connected with the town sewer'*, and in November 1883 they wrote again asking permission for the well to be used for flushing the sewers with the aid of a storage tank. The Managers agreed providing they received a nominal rent of 1/- (5p) per year and:

'that if it be thought advisable to build the tank within the boundary wall of the playground such tank sh^d be available for use in case of fire without charge and that it be covered in securely so as not to interfere with the use of the playground.'

In the same Minutes, the problem of ventilating the classrooms was raised, and two sash windows and ventilators were ordered. The Sanitary Inspector, Mr. Charles Gander agreed to oversee the work. Unfortunately, the subject of ventilation keeps cropping up in the minutes and logbooks for over twenty years.

In 1884, following a report from Mr. Gander, the Managers decided:

'to insert two windows in each of the Class rooms in the Boys & Girls' Schools.'

In June 1887, Mr. Gardner wrote:

'This week I have adopted the plan of allowing the boys to have their Reading lessons in the yard, the atmosphere of the room being very close.'

In the Infants' School, the Government Inspectors were unhappy that a room which should have been used for instruction was used as a Cloakroom. In 1889, it was reported:

'The ventilation of the class-room needs attention, hats and cloaks must be removed from it.'

Nothing was done, so the following year the Inspector reported, rather ambiguously:

'Hats and cloaks are still in the Cloak Room which is full enough without them. Unless these are removed I shall be unable to report another year that this room is properly furnished for Infants.'

The building of a new room was begun in October 1891, though the children were still at school and thus distracted from their work. An extra window had been put into the Infants' department and Miss Clark was very pleased as:

'The new window in the class room is a great improvement as far as ventilation is concerned.'

In December 1893:

'It was thought that if an additional door were opened from the Infants' Class Room into the playground it would improve the ventilation.'

In 1894:

> *'The "Babies" Class is getting too large for the Class Room, the ventilation being so very imperfect during the hot weather therefore the classes spend as much time as possible on the playground.'*

Major work was carried out during the summer break of 1895, but it was unfinished by the time the school reopened on September 3rd. Miss Clark reported:

> *'Reopened school on Monday morning, but was obliged to close again until Tuesday as the schoolroom was not ready for use. It is impossible to work according to the Time Table, as until the class room is finished building, all the children must be accommodated in one room.'*

There were, at the time, almost 140 children in the Infants' department.
On September 20th:

> *'The Classroom still remains unfinished consequently the general work is greatly interfered with. Most of the lessons have had to be given in the schoolroom this week.'*

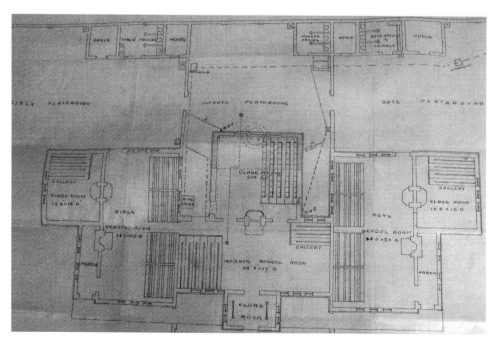

Plans for the enlargement of the Infants' Department in 1895.

The completed school and school houses, which remained almost unchanged externally until its demolition in 1988.

The work was finally finished at the end of September, the Infants' School being closed for two days for cleaning.

Further time was lost in October when desks were installed instead of the benches previously used. Unfortunately, the seats had not arrived, so they were of very little use for some time.

In July 1901:

'Mr Gardner complained of the inadequate ventilation of the Boys' Schoolroom. The Secretary was directed to have a ventilator placed at each gable end of the room.'

In March 1902:

'Dr. Smith and Dr Browne with Mr Henderson were appointed a subcommittee to see to the ventilation of the Boys' School.'

On May 19th 1903:

'Two gentlemen called and took an Inventory of the School furniture on behalf of the Warwickshire County Council.'

Chapter 8

OTHER FINANCIAL MATTERS

As well as problems with the School Building Fund, the Managers had great difficulty in keeping the bank account of the general school funds in credit.

In addition to salaries, there were general maintenance costs, and purchases to be made for the schools. Early on, the Master and Mistress appear to have bought items for the schools and presented bills to the Managers haphazardly. Teachers applied annually for a raise in salary. Sometimes this was granted, sometimes not. There was no standard scale and few formal qualifications, and occasionally jobs were advertised at different rates, according to supply and demand.

School income was from pupil fees, Government grant and subscriptions, and some grant aid for specific items from the Worcester Archidiaconal Council.

Fees, or 'school pence', were paid according to the number of children attending school. Modifications were made in the fees in 1877, when it was agreed that, per week:

> *'Halftimers to pay 3d – no reduction unless there be more than 2 children in a department of the Schools – Children of Tradesmen to pay 6d & 4d.*
> *NB The Teacher to be instructed to submit to the Committee a list of admissions during the previous month in order that the proper fees be assigned.*
> *   That if a child who has made the requisite number of attendances during the School year be absent (except on account of illness) on the day of the visit of H.M. Inspector the fee for that child during the next year be double the ordinary fee.'*

In 1887, a scheme was introduced to encourage regular school attendance. The Managers decided that a percentage of the fees paid should be returned in cash for unbroken attendance. In 1891 school fees were abolished and replaced by a Government School Fee Grant. To make up the deficit after this date, parents were asked to pay 1/- (5p) or 2/6 (22½p) a quarter.

The Government grant was dependent on the annual report of H.M. Inspector, and varied from year to year. Basically, the amount depended on the average school attendance, which was not the same as the number of pupils registered, plus examination results in Reading, Writing and Arithmetic. Extra money was paid for passes in Literature, Grammar and Geography until these became regular lessons in the school.

It was the responsibility of the Managers to check that the pupil registers were kept correctly. This was done on a regular basis, usually by the Rev. A.H. Williams or his curate – first the Rev. Charles J.F. Yule (1885-88), then Rev. Onebye R. Walker (1889), followed by Rev. Charles Francis Trusted (1890), Rev. Cyril Price (1893), Rev. D. Davenport (1897), Rev. E.F. Lipscomb (1898), Rev. R.J. Abbott (1898) and Rev. Joseph Sumner (1901).

There were also regular visits by the Rector, Rev. Alfred H. Williams, or one of his Curates, and a few by the Attendance Officer, William Cook, to inspect the school registers, checking the names marked against those children actually in the school. There is only one occasion recorded when they were found to be incorrect. In February 1894:

'Tested the registers and found them correct except for one slight inaccuracy.'

This was signed by Rev. Cyril Price, a Curate at St. Nicholas' Church. On the following day, the Infants' Mistress, Miss Clark, wrote an explanation for the error:

'The inaccuracy referred to was Ethel Winfield (a baby) marked present; but the number on the Registers and "Present at all" were the same owing to Charles Bayliss being marked absent and counted as present.'

The new Schools had been built to accommodate 300 children, but in June 1878 there were 396 children on the books, with an average attendance of 305.

Because of the importance of attendance numbers, parents of pupils being absent on the day of the Inspector's visit could be fined. In 1876 a pupil called Jane Adcock had been kept away from the Alcester Schools and sent to a private school, resulting in a loss of grant. The Managers resolved that in:

'similar cases an extra fee of 1d a week be exacted until such time as the child had earned a grant for the School.'

The Government grant could be, and was, reduced by a number of other factors – too few teachers, too many children in one room or inadequate lighting, heating and ventilation. In 1893 the Inspector reported an insufficiency of 'out offices' [lavatories].

The Managers were constantly trying to balance the books, and failing. The Managers agreed an overdraft with the Bill Banking Company, with two of their number agreeing to be guarantors, but this resulted in further deficits due to bank charges.

Things came to a head in 1884 when the Managers had a year-end deficit of £284. They considered removing the schools from the Voluntary system and becoming a Board School. This could have resulted in the Marquis of Hertford reclaiming the land on which the Schools were built. Fortunately the Government grant for that year was £236 and they agreed to continue the schools for another year.

A special meeting was called to consider the financial situation. The overdraft was £311, and the bank agreed to extend the limit to £400. A canvass for subscriptions was unsatisfactory, and it was foreseen that after receipt of the Government grant there would still be a deficit of about £150. The only solution was to reduce the teaching staff to the minimum allowed by Government.

Three members of staff were given notice to quit.

In 1885 *'it appeared probable that the expenditure of the schools for the year would not exceed the receipts. This was in consequence of the diminution of the Staff of Teachers. This was considered satisfactory.'*

To give them due credit, as soon as money was available the Managers did employ more teaching assistants.

The balance sheet for 1886 showed that expenditure had exceeded income by only £20 – £16 of which was owing to bank charges. A Bazaar was held.

High St., Alcester, 1904, Corn Exchange in centre.

This was no ordinary Bazaar as we might imagine today. According to the Alcester Chronicle, for four days, from Thursday 8th December to Monday 13th, not including Sunday, the ground floor of the Corn Exchange in Alcester High Street was transformed to depict an old fashioned shopping street. Different items were displayed for sale in the various Tudor-style black-and-white 'shops'. One of the shops was run by the Marquis and Marchioness of Hertford, another by the Rector, his wife and daughter. One of the local ladies walked along the 'street' selling floral buttonholes and posies.

There were entertainments such as a 'fortune-telling postmistress', an 'electro-biological' entertainment which caused boys to do exactly as they were told(!), a 'fishing lake', recitations and an exhibition of 'wax-work figures' who were local boys, with a narration by a Mrs. Jarley. There was also an auction.

Upstairs, it was possible to look down on the 'happenings' below whilst enjoying refreshments and performances by the local choir and Wilkes' Band from Redditch.

The Managers wrote to the local press, thanking all who had helped to raise the sum of £334-14-6. At today's values, this would be over £20,000, which enabled the Managers to discharge the bank overdraft and continue running the school.

This did not end the problems, as maintenance and redecoration of the buildings, staff salary increases, and changes to the classrooms all added to the expenses.

The balance sheet at the end of 1893 showed another deficit of over £206 including more bank charges. In the Infants' School, Miss Clark had been pleased to receive a number of forms (benches) which could be used as additional desks, as well as window blinds and a mat. A Rummage sale and social teas had raised over £30. The teachers were:

'thanked for their care in economising the expenditure.'

In 1895 it was found necessary to enlarge the Infants' School. The estimated cost was £101.2.4 for the Building & £11 for Gallery & desks.

'It was proposed by Mr T.H. Smith, seconded by Mr T. Averill and carried unanimously that the money be borrowed from the Bank and that an effort be made in the spring to clear it off.'

More desks were provided in 1898 and Miss Clark recorded:

'The new desks were placed on the Gallery on Friday (Nov 25) and have proved very useful already.'

In 1896:

> 'Mr. Henderson asked permission to order two additional trucks of Lickey gravel for the Boys' play Ground and to insert a grating & drain in the corner of the playground to take off the surface water. Also, to erect a small shed in Infants' ground for coal etc.'

This expenditure was granted, but not the request in the same Minutes for an increase in salary for the Infants' Mistress.

In February 1900, Miss Clark had written:

> 'We have been unable to use our Class Room for several mornings until quite late owing to the intense cold. This winter the room has rarely been really warm enough for Babies.'

Similar comments had been recorded during each winter since the new Classroom had been added. During the Christmas break of 1900-1901 a new stove was put into the Infants' classroom and was much appreciated:

> 'The stove in the Class Room will be of great benefit as the room can now be made really warm.'

It was just as well that the stove had been installed as, during the same holiday, the school had been flooded and took a month to dry out.

Another stove was installed in the main Infant schoolroom the following winter, and again Miss Clark was appreciative:

> 'The new stove which has been placed in the schoolroom makes the room much more comfortable to work in... The schoolroom is much warmer now than it ever has been, the stove proving a great success.'

Chapter 9

THE MANAGERS

The Reverend Alfred Henry Williams, Rector of St. Nicholas' Church, Alcester, from 1869 to 1907, was probably the most important character in driving the development of the schools. The Church of England was responsible for the original school in Alcester and Rev. Williams chaired the Management Committee overseeing its enlargement and alteration and the building of the school houses in 1871.

Town 'worthies', who were also involved with St. Nicholas' Church, were willing to give their time and energy into not only attending Managers' Meetings but organising aspects of the running of the Schools.

When trying to raise funds to rebuild the Schools, Managers were given areas of the town to visit, knock on

Rev. Alfred Henry Williams.

doors and ask for subscriptions. They were required to have plans drawn up, advertise for tenders and ensure the work was carried out satisfactorily. Each year they had to consider what they could afford to spend on salaries and hire and fire school staff. There were several occasions when they had to act as judge and jury regarding complaints made against Teachers.

There were two cases for the Managers to consider in 1885. In October they had to:

> *'consider the case of two boys J & G. Baylis who had been refused readmission by the Master in consequence of their having been taken away during School hours by the mother in defiance of the Master and in consequence of the mother's insulting language.'*

Mr. Phillip's entry in the Logbook for September 4th states:

> '*Mrs W Bayliss, The Moors, Alcester, not only deliberately walked into my schoolroom at 4.40 pm on Monday last & ordered her two boys (John & George) to leave the room, notwithstanding my orders to the contrary, but she also grossly insulted & abused me, in consequence of which, I have every day since refused to readmit them until she offers a sufficient apology.*'

The boys were refused entry to the school on several occasions throughout September and October.

On Nov 17th:

> '*J & G Bayliss again presented themselves morning & afternoon but as the mother still refuses to apologise they were again refused admission notwithstanding a threatening letter from Mr. Ansell, Solicitor, Birmingham.*'

The Managers took legal advice from the Education Department in London, and the result was that:

> '*the Master was justified in keeping them in after the general body of the School was dismissed – and also in refusing them readmission into the Schools without an apology from the mother, after she had forcibly withdrawn them with the use of abusive language.*'

In November a Special Meeting was called:

> '*in consequence of a serious breach of discipline having been committed by R. Booker who was suspended from attendance at school until the Master had received instructions from the Managers.*
> *The case as stated set forth that R. Booker when under punishment by Mr. Phillip had produced a large stone from his pocket which he was in the act of throwing at the Master when his hand was seized by an assistant teacher who had observed his intention.*'

The boy's mother:

> '*was informed that R. Booker would be received back into the school only on the condition of his submitting to a public caning to be administered by the Master before the school and in presence of two of the school managers.*'

Mr. Phillip's version in the logbook reads:

'Richard Booker a 3rd class boy was suspended, pending instructions from the Managers for wilfully & persistently refusing to obey orders & afterwards aggravating the offence by attempting to hit the master with a large stone.'

In January 1886, Mr Phillip:

'Refused to admit R Booker as his parents object to his being punished.'

The case was taken to the Magistrates' Court, who laid down conditions for the boy's re-admittance to the school. On February 15th 1886 it is recorded:

'John Booker came down to the school this morning with his son Richard and having promised to comply with the conditions laid down by the Managers at their Meeting on the 30th of Nov last the boy was re-admitted & during the course of the forenoon he submitted to a public caning (consisting of 6 strokes on the back) in the presence of the Rev C J Yule & Dr T H Smith, two of the Managers.'

This was not the end of the matter, however, as the boy's mother:

'came down to the school a few minutes after 12 & finding all her efforts to forcibly enter the room & take away her son were in vain she shook the door violently for several minutes. She then became most abusive & used most insulting language before a large number of children upon which the Master, in the presence of Mrs. Bates ordered her to leave the premises which she did after a moments consideration.'

During 1891 Mrs. Bates received a letter:

Alcester Jan 26. 1891

Madam,

My attention has been drawn to a child sent to your school this morning named Florence Tustin whom you beat unmercifully without any provocation whatever you must know how far you have exceeded your duty as Mistress in this matter.

I wish on behalf of her mother (Mrs. Tustin) to inform you that unless you apologise to her for the ill treatment given this morning and promise you will not abuse the child again in similar manner a summons against you will be taken out for the offence.

Yrs sin

W. Burdett

When the Managers investigated, Mrs. Bates informed them that:

> *'the only punishment which the child received was two boxes on the ear for stubbornness in refusing to answer a question.'*

Mr. Burdett agreed that he had been misinformed, having had the story third hand, and he was told to apologise to Mrs. Bates.

In 1897, a meeting had been convened:

> *'to investigate certain charges of cruelty brought against the Teachers in the Boys and Infants Departments in respect to some Workhouse children attending the Schools.... The enquiry occupied two hours during which time the parents of the children, the Master of the Workhouse, the Matron's Assistant and the Teachers were examined.'*

The result of the inquiry was that the charges of cruelty were proved to be groundless and a full report was published in the Alcester Chronicle.

The Rector, Rev. A.H. Williams, was also involved directly with the children in the school. He visited the school on a regular basis to take classes in Scripture, and could see for himself the poor standard of teaching and discipline of Mr. Sayce. During Mr. Phillip's tenure, he continued to visit, but on an irregular basis, supplementing the Scripture teaching, especially before the annual visit of the Diocesan Inspector. Later, his Curates took on much of his responsibility for scripture lessons.

Rev. Williams provided prizes for boys' examination results, and tried to encourage more regular attendance. In July 1875, the Master reported that:

> *'the Rev A H Williams & Mr. Averill* (another Manager) *visited the school shortly after 11 o'clock on Friday in order to present the 3 most deserving boys with a mathematical box of instruments each & likewise pay 4d per subject to all those boys who passed in more than one subject on Wednesday last...*
>
> *The Rector having examined the passes on the Schedule pointed out to the boys that those who had attended the greatest number of times had invariably passed the most creditably & therefore urged all present to attend school as regularly as possible during the ensuing year.'*

Rev. Williams also showed concern for the poorer pupils in the school. In January 1879 he:

'expressed a wish that all those children who seemed to be suffering from want of food should at once be supplied with bread & butter.' In February he *'again visited the school on Tuesday & ordered the school fees to be remitted in cases of great poverty.'*

The Marquis and Marchioness of Hertford took an active interest in the Schools. The Marquis, too, provided prizes for the boys in Scripture, Reading, Dictation and Arithmetic. His wife provided prizes for the girls in needlework. At the end of 1876, these prizes were presented by the Marchioness at the Corn Exchange, in Alcester High Street. On January 8th 1877 the Marchioness visited the school and:

'promised the children a treat on the occasion of Lady Georgina's Marriage which is arranged to take place on Tuesday the 23rd January.'

In 1891 the Government changed the method of funding for schools, and the Managers opted to take the Fee Grant, which meant that pupils no longer needed to pay the 'school pennies'. It also meant that parents did not need to keep their children out of school when they could not afford to pay, though exercise books still had to be provided.

Under the Voluntary Schools Act of 1897, the Managers decided to become a Voluntary Aided School and:

'That the Church School Association for the Diocese of Worcester be and the same is hereby nominated the association to which this school proposes to belong.'

The relationship between the Managers and the staff at the schools seems to have been, on the whole, friendly and co-operative. However there was an incident in 1891 in which Mr. Gardner and the Chairman of the Managers, the Rev. A.H. Williams had a disagreement. For some reason, unknown to Mr. Gardner, the Infants were not immediately sent up into the Boys' School on the first day of the school year (November 1st) as usual.

Three weeks later, when they had been sent up, Mr. Gardner judged that four boys were 'totally unfit to come into the Boys Room' and sent them back to the Infants. The Infants' Mistress then spoke to the Managers and:

'The Rector visited the school & informed me [Mr. Gardner] that the four boys above mentioned were to be admitted, all my objections being put aside.'

The following day, Mr. Gardner admitted Ernest Tarver, Geo Green, Albert Panter and James Harrison. He was not happy about this because:

'The three former were sent out of the Infants' 2nd Class, the latter out of the 3rd. This will necessitate the formation of an extra Class, besides the seven Standards.'

In 1902 a further Education Act, known as the Butler Act, would take much of the pressure off the shoulders of the Managers as the first Local Education Authorities were set up. In 1903, Warwickshire Education Authority took over much of the responsibility for many of the schools in the County. Because Alcester was classified as a Voluntary Aided School, rather than a County-controlled School, the Managers still had a say in the finance and staffing but standardised salary scales were set up and teachers no longer needed to apply annually to the Managers for increases.

In his Annual Report in 1903, the Chairman, Rev. Alfred H. Williams wrote:

'With July came in a new system under the Education Act of 1902. Since that date the management has passed very largely out of the hands of the local managers to an Education Committee of the County Council. It remains to be proved whether the centralization of the work of education in the county will be for better or worse. Henceforward the financing of the schools will depend on the Education Committee, and the local managers will be relieved from this anxiety. They will, however, still be liable for the maintenance of the buildings and the enlargement of them, should that be deemed necessary, towards which they will have the rent of the teachers' houses. Anything beyond this must be met by subscription. Happily the Managers retain in their hands the control of the religious education given in the Schools and the appointment of teachers, so that we may hope that in these Schools the children of Christian parents will continue to receive Christian teaching imparted by Christian teachers. For this we have striven for many years, devoting much time and thought to the economical management of the Schools, and to the raising of sufficient funds to maintain them in efficiency. We cannot in the future expect them to be managed as economically. We must be satisfied if they are kept up to an equal or higher standard of efficiency, and turn out well-instructed scholars, good Christians, and good citizens.'

Chapter 10

THE TEACHING STAFF

There were three levels of 'teachers' involved in the schools – the Master (Boys' School) or Mistress (Girls' School and Infants' School), Assistant Teachers and Pupil Teachers and they could be assisted by Monitors or Monitresses. The first Master, Mr. Sayce, was not the only one who left under a cloud (Chapter 2).

The second Master, Mr. John Phillip, who served from 1871 to 1886 was asked to resign after being expelled from the local lodge of the Oddfellows Society. He moved to Northamptonshire with his wife, Jane, and their children. The Phillips had a total of 13 children, and Mr. Phillip also served as organist in St. Nicholas' Church in Alcester.

A letter from a possible new employer asking the reason why Mr. Phillip resigned was answered as follows:

'The reason why Mr. Phillip left our schools was because he had become involved in some monetary difficulties and irregularities (unconnected with the schools) which in the opinion of the Managers placed him in a position incompatible with the continuance of his duties.'

Mr. William Gardner was also an organist in the Church. He became Master of the Boys' School in 1886 and continued until 1922, guiding the school through many changes of personnel and regulations, and financial ups and downs. Not only was he teaching at the school, but his wife, Jane, served as an Assistant Teacher and a Supply Teacher; his son, Evan, became a probationary teacher, and one of his daughters, Evelyn, was a monitress before becoming a pupil teacher in the Girls' School. She later became Head Teacher of Great Alne Primary School.

In the Girls' School, the first Mistress, Miss Lucy Walsingham, lasted less than a year under the new regulations of the 1870 Education Act, but Mrs. Fanny E. Bates, a Government Certificated Teacher, appointed in 1871, proved to be an excellent appointment and stayed at the school for 27 years as Mistress.

Married women were not usually employed at this time, but Mrs. Bates was a widow. She arrived in Alcester with an 11 year old daughter, Kate, and a 9 year old son, Arthur, who died in 1874, aged only 12. Other single women employed as teachers were obliged to resign their positions on getting married.

The Gardner family outside the School House.

Mrs. Bates was followed in 1899 by Miss Mary Thornley, who resigned in 1923 to facilitate the merging of the Boys' and Girls' schools to make one mixed school. The Managers were very appreciative of her offer, and agreed to her one condition – that she be retained as an Assistant Teacher until the end of 1924.

There were no 'supply' teachers until the 1900s and when Mr. Phillip became ill in 1877, Rev. A.H. Williams wrote in the logbook:

'During the last ten days the school has been carried on by the P[upil]T[eacher] under the superintendence of the Rector, as the Master was unable to attend owing to Sickness.'

Mrs. Bates' daughter, Kate, helped her mother when required, and later became a teacher herself; William Gardner's wife, Jane, also helped out, as did Mrs. Sayce in the early years.

The Infants' School was staffed by Assistant Teachers until 1879, when it was ordered to be split from the upper Schools and staffed separately by Government Certificated teachers. Miss Mary Carter was Mistress from 1881 to 1883, and was followed by Mary L. Clark who remained for almost 40 years. One of her first entries in the logbook was:

'The children seem to be in a very backward condition and attend very irregularly.'

Like Mrs. Bates in the Girls' School, Miss Clark in the Infants' School found difficulty with the poor staffing. In May 1884, she wrote:

'*The Time Table cannot be strictly adhered to, as there is an insufficient staff, only Mistress and Monitor. Average attendance for the week 107.*'

By the end of May, things had not improved as the numbers went up to 121, with the Mistress and Monitor, Annie Cull, being the only staff. By July of 1884, the numbers on the books had gone up to 144.

After the Summer holidays an Assistant Mistress, Miss Leigh, was employed. In November, the beginning of the new school year, the older children were moved up to the Boys' and Girls' schools and the Infant numbers dropped to below 100. Because of this reduction in numbers, Annie Cull was dismissed, '*the decrease in the attendance rendering it unnecessary to retain her services.*' Miss Leigh was employed only until the end of the year, when she was replaced by Miss Mary J. Cooper, who transferred from the Girls' School. Miss Clark records a pleasing improvement in the children's work under the tutelage of Miss Cooper. Miss Leigh returned in February 1885 to help out at the school as a voluntary assistant.

Miss Clark was determined to do the best for her Infants, and asked the Managers to provide extra help for the "Babies" – the 3-year-olds – '*it being impossible to teach them satisfactorily as part of another class.*' The Government Inspector also suggested that the 'Baby-room' should be enlarged. A monitress, Annie Ford, was employed in May 1885.

Mary Clark is not reticent in recording her praise for the staff in her school. In July 1885, she recorded:

'*The Babies under Miss Leigh are improving satisfactorily,*' and '*a very successful lesson on Lath Plaiting was given by Miss Cooper on Wednesday afternoon.*'

A large number of Assistant Teachers came and went during the 32 years when the Schools were run solely by the Managers.

Among those in the Girls' and Infants' Schools were Miss Gertrude M. Airey (1901-03), Kate Bates (1879-95), Alma Chambers (1900), Lily Cook (1895), Mary J. Cooper (1883-1921), Miss Lilian Crump (1899-1900), Miss Edwins (?-1897), Miss Fewstie (1897-98), Alice Maud Gray (1895-1899 then 1900-1903), Florence Griffiths (1900), Alice Hoy (1876-80), Alice Jones (1897), Miss Knight (1883), Miss Lawson (1895), Kate Louisa Leigh (1884-85), May Page (1900), Hannah Rigg (1900), Jesse Tee (1899), Hannah Tunnicliffe (1897-1900) and Miss Wood (1895 for a month).

For the Boys' School, the Minutes and Logbook mention Mr. W. J. Addis (1878), William John Barkwill (1900-1901), Mr. J. Beattie (1886), Joe Downing Breffit (1887-90), William Chatterley (1901-02), Thomas Dodson (1884), Charles Thornton Howes (1887-88), Henry Charles Lawsdale (1895-96), Joseph Vaughan Lloyd (1891-?), Mr. W. C. Lloyd (1885), Mr. Selvage (1885), Mr. H. Singleton (1886-87), Wilfred J. Slade (1902-04), George Herbert Smith (1875-1884), Mr. Stradling (?-1892), Henry John Tench (1890-91) and Martin Frederick Whiting (1896-1899).

As can be seen from the dates, some stayed for several years, some just a short time. Several moved on to College or to other posts. In 1878, Mr. W. J. Addis 'Ex-pupil Teacher from Madley Nat. School commenced duties as Assistant Master for 3 months.' Mr. Thomas Dodson, 'whose work has proved altogether unsatisfactory,' lasted from May to July 1884 and 'was called upon to resign his post as Assistant Master.'

Kate, Mrs. Fanny Bates' daughter, helped out at the school when required before becoming a qualified Assistant Teacher. She is recorded in 1901 as a Teacher of Cookery living in Croydon, Surrey, with her retired mother. In the same year Alma Chambers, from Handsworth, Staffordshire, and Hannah Rigg from Whitehaven, Cumberland, were both boarders at the home of Frederick Boswell in Henley Street. They were both employed after the resignation of Miriam Fanny Tunnicliffe. Miss Tunnicliffe was obliged to resign before she married Harry Baggott Johnson, a Dispensing Chemist. In 1911 she was an Assistant Mistress living with her husband and two children in Ladywood, Birmingham.

Lily Cook, who had been trained at Great Alne Mixed School, stayed less than a year, but in 1911 was Mistress of her own school in Tockenham, near Wooton Bassett, Wiltshire. In her employ as Assistant Mistress was her sister Elsie Arrowsmith Cook. Their older sister, Ellen, kept house for them both.

Miss Fewstie found a post at Minchinhampton; Alice Hoy had to leave when the Infants' Department was ordered to be staffed by Certificated Teachers; Alice Jones was dismissed for inefficiency; Miss Knight was dismissed for inefficiency and insubordination. Alice Gray served several periods at the school, sometimes standing in when other teachers were ill, particularly in the Infants' School. An older sister and a brother were also teachers. In 1911 Alice was still living with her parents in Cow Honeybourne near Evesham.

Kate Louisa Leigh served as a voluntary assistant in the Infants' School for over a year, then moved to Birmingham, later becoming a Diocesan Mission worker. She died in 1960, aged 95. Jessie Tee, though appointed to the Infants' School, did not take up the appointment.

Mr. Selvage and Mr. Stradling were both dismissed for insubordination; Mr. Howes and Henry Singleton left to go to Training Colleges; Wilfred Slade went to Saltley Training College and in 1911 was a '*College trained elementary teacher*' living in Stechford, Birmingham. Henry Tench went to a post in Dudley.

Pupil Teachers were appreciated for a number of years, and had to sign indentures. They were trained on the job to become Articled Teachers and could progress further up the teaching ladder. The Schools were given extra money for training such pupils who started their apprenticeship at the age of 14.

Those mentioned in the Minutes and Logbook are Samuel Hartles (1867-71), Tom Colling (1871-1875), Byron Hill (1880), Claude Phillip (1882-1885), Emily M. Sisam (1887-89), George Herbert Smith (1875-80) and Martin Frederick Whiting (1894-96) – both of whom became Assistant Teachers.

Sam Hartles was dismissed in 1871. In the 1881 census he is recorded as a butcher, employing one man, in Swan Street, Alcester. Tom Colling completed his apprenticeship in December 1875 when he '*left School having served his apprenticeship very creditably & to the entire satisfaction of Master & Managers.*' But in the 1881 census, he is employed as a Commercial Clerk in the leather industry in Camberwell, London.

Herbert Smith arrived at the school in May of 1875 '*having passed his examination as a candidate in January last at the Alveston Nat School.*' He was not as successful as Tom Colling, having to be reprimanded for lateness. In March 1876, Mr. Phillip recorded:

> '*Pupil Teacher Herbert Smith in spite of many warnings & threatening is still most unpunctual at his lessons. During the whole of this last month he was only 4 times present at the appointed time viz 8 am. Generally speaking he does not arrive till 8.10 & frequently not till 8.15.*'

And again on January 19th 1877:

> '*Pupil Teacher G H Smith has been unpunctual at his lessons this week. On Wednesday & Thursday mornings he was 25 minutes late & on Friday 10 minutes late.*'

Late he might have been, but his work was praised by Her Majesty's Inspector in the end-of-year report for 1877: '*G H Smith has passed well.*' He became the Assistant Master of the school, but in 1884, he left the school to '*sail to America*'.

Mr. William Gardner was impressed with Joe Breffit. After being ill for two weeks, he wrote:

> '*During my absence ... the school was left in charge of J.D. Breffit Assistant, who carried on the work in an efficient manner.*'

Unfortunately, when Mr. Breffit left the school in 1890, attempts to find another ex-pupil teacher to replace him proved very difficult and Mrs. Jane Gardner was employed temporarily as Assistant in the Boys' School from 18th November to 8th December. The new Assistant, Henry John Tench, lasted only five months, and there was a gap of another month before another appointment was made.

Claude Phillip had his indentures cancelled as he was judged, by his father, to be 'unsatisfactory'. I am told by a descendant that he later joined the Navy, but he is recorded in the 1901 census as a labourer in the gem trade in Birmingham, and in 1911 as a storekeeper in the Royal Small Arms Factory in Enfield, Middlesex.

In the 1891 census, Emily Sisam, stepdaughter to carpenter William Hunt of Henley Street, is recorded as a Salvation Army Officer. She died, still single, in 1933.

Fred Whiting became an Assistant Teacher and eventually left the school in 1899 for a post as Assistant Master at Holy Trinity, Coventry. In 1903 he was Headmaster of Helmstead School in Essex.

Below these were Monitors and Monitresses. These were pupils beyond school leaving age, usually 14, who assisted the teachers in various ways, including supervising other pupils in their work. Sometimes they were put in charge of a whole class or group of children, similar to a Teaching Assistant today, but their employment usually lasted for a year. Certainly this is what happened in the Infants' School.

Some of the youngsters are recorded in the 1890s as 'Candidate for Pupil Teacher', so they worked at the school to gain experience before being assessed by the Government Inspector to see if they were suitable to embark on an apprenticeship as a Pupil Teacher.

Monitors and Monitresses were paid a small amount per week for their duties. Many are mentioned by name in the minutes and logbooks, particularly those of the Infants' School – Eliza Bates (1900-03), Gertrude Boddington (1893-94), Fred Burdett (1899), William Burrage (1877), Constance Cook (1899-1900), Annie Cull (1883), Alfred Cull (1884), Ernest Dexter (1886), Charlotte Farr (1895-99), Annie Ford (1885), Emma Gorle (1887-88), Eva Helens (1890-91), Eleanor Higgins (1889), Alice Jones (1892-95 – see also above), Thomas William Meusing (1878), Kate Pepper (1891-92), Annie Phillip, daughter of the Master John Phillip (1883-84), Edith Russell (1897), Alice Shrimpton (1900), Eleanor Shrimpton (1901), Florence Skinner (1889 for three months), Gertrude Skinner (1894 for four months), Rose Skinner (1889-90), Eliza Jane Smith (1892), Albert Tompkins (1887), Eva Tompkins (1886-87), Alice Wheeler (1900), Fred Whiting (1886 – see also above), Lillie Wright (1891-93).

Born in Cheshire, Eliza Bates was staying with her aunts in Dunnington while she served a Monitress. Gertrude Boddington was the granddaughter of the local Vaccination Officer and left to 'a situation in Birmingham'. According to the 1901 census, Fred Burdett had become a Solicitor's Clerk and died, still in Alcester, in 1936 aged 53. Also in 1901, Alfred Cull was a Railway Guard living in Whitnash, Warwickshire. His sister, Annie Cull, became a Grocer's Clerk in Alcester before moving to London to become a Hotel Manageress in the Strand. She later set up as a dressmaker and according to the 1911 Census, she was still single and visiting friends in Hendon, Middlesex.

Ernest Dexter moved to Birmingham and became a milk deliveryman, then a worker at a chemical works. At the age of 37 in 1911 he is recorded as a widowed cycle enameller and a patient at All Saints Hospital in Winson Green. Charlotte Farr became a tailoress, before marrying Cuthbert Downs Wellum in 1908 and moving to Deritend, Birmingham. Emma Gorle was considered by Miss Clark to be 'too harsh with her little ones' and her conduct 'unsatisfactory'. She married a railway signalman, Samuel Ferris, and in 1911 was living in Bristol. Eva Helens stayed only two months before leaving the town 'for an indefinite period'.

Eleanor Higgins became a domestic servant in Birmingham, before setting up as a dressmaker. She moved back to live with her family in Worcestershire, still working as a dressmaker, as did two of her sisters. She died in 1947, aged 73. Kate Pepper moved to Gloucestershire and became a dressmaker before marrying Henry James Perkins in 1902. In 1884 Annie Phillip 'failed to pass the Government Examination for Candidates.' This meant that she could not sign up for an apprenticeship as a Pupil Teacher and her employment came to an end in April 1884.

Rose Skinner was well thought of by Miss Clark; at the end of her term of employment she went to London. But Miss Clark thought 'E.J. Smith does not show any aptitude for teaching little ones'. She left in the autumn of 1892, 'her services being required at home.'

Albert Tompkins became a printer's compositor in Alcester and married Eliza Ellen, otherwise known as 'Nellie'. He died in Alcester in 1945 aged 71. In 1891 his sister Eva was a domestic servant in Charlbury, Oxfordshire. Lillian Wright started well, but was later considered 'of very little use amongst the babies' [the 3-year-olds]. She married decorator Thomas Walter Cobley in 1908 and in 1911 was living in Rugby. She died in Northamptonshire aged 81.

Chapter 11

THE PUPILS

Pupils at the Schools came from a variety of backgrounds. There were other schools in the town, including the Grammar School Preparatory school at Birch Abbey, but these were fee-paying, and were more expensive than the National Schools. Even so, all parents were expected to pay the 'school pence' and later provide copy books or exercise books for their children. There was a sliding scale of 'pence' whereby children of poorer families paid less than those from a higher class such as prominent tradesmen.

Even those living in the workhouse were expected to pay their way, though their school fees were paid for by the Union Guardians. In April 1887, Mr. Gardner records, *'Mr. Cook, Relieving Officer, paid the School Fees (£3.9s.6d) owed by the Guardians for the half year ending March 28th 1887.'* There was a discount for the second and subsequent children. Families tended to be large – even the headmaster Mr. John Phillip had thirteen children, many of whom attended the School.

In December 1881, the school fees were reduced, *'the Committee having decided that all children under 5 years of age shall attend school for one penny per week. All scholars heretofore have paid 2d per week.'* Then in September 1891, the Free Education Act came into force, so that school fees were no longer charged.

Although expected to go out to work as young as possible, children between the ages of 3 and 13 were obliged to attend school for 10 hours per week. Depending on their working hours, this might be mornings or afternoons, and made the job of teaching rather difficult.

In 1880, the Elementary Education Act (Mundella's Act) made school compulsory between the ages of 5 and 10. The school leaving age was raised to 11 in 1893, then to 12 in 1899. Children were still admitted to school from the age of 3 – this lowest age grouping was usually referred to as the 'Babies' class.

At some times of the year, notably in the summer and autumn, children were expected to help out with harvesting fruit, vegetables, grain and hay. There are many entries in the logbook bemoaning the fact that many children were absent in order to help in these activities and so earn money for their families.

The workhouse children, usually referred to as Union children, were poorly dressed and shod, as were many from the poorer areas of the town such as

Bleachfield Street early 1900s.

Bleachfield Street. It was here that many workers in the needle industry lived in small terraced houses. It was not unusual for ten or more people to live in each house. On wet days these children might not attend school.

The Union children had a poor record of attendance. On several occasions, it seems as if a concerted decision was made by someone in the workhouse to keep the children away from school. On February 8th 1888, '*All the Union children have been absent since the holidays,*' and on 22nd, '*The Union boys, seven in number, have not put in an appearance since the holidays, this being the seventh week of their abstention.*' They finally returned on February 27th, with no explanation.

The Alcester Poor Law Union was made up of 22 parishes, including some in Worcestershire, and included 29 workhouses. Alcester's Workhouse was on Kinwarton Road. In 1881 it had 131 residents. It was converted in 1984 into Oversley House (residential accommodation). The Workhouse infirmary became Alcester Hospital, demolished in 2011.

There were instances of communicable diseases and conditions such as lice and ringworm which affected these children more than others as they lived more closely together. There are also records of children being sent home from school because of their '*uncleanliness*'.

There were two recorded incidents when teachers were accused of cruelty to workhouse children (see Chapter 9) but on both occasions the members of staff were totally exonerated.

Oversley House 2012.

Most of the children attending the schools are anonymous. Individual children are usually mentioned because of their achievements, for example winning prizes, or for causing problems. (See Chapter 11) Some are mentioned when they leave school to start work, or when they are admitted to the school other than at the start of a term. Recognisable among the names are some whose families still live in Alcester.

Charles Bayliss (Gashouse Lane) won a scholarship to the Grammar School in 1876 and was given an award for distinguished Army service in 1917. Herbert Bayliss (Bleachfield Street), on the other hand, was punished for truancy and spending his school pence in 1875; and another family – John and George Bayliss (The Moors) – were, with their parents, the subject of court proceedings and expulsion in 1885.

Early prizewinners were from the Cull, Ellins, Gittus, Haywood, Moore, Skinner, Stanley and Whiting families; Thomas Blackband, Claude Phillip and Frank Skinner won scholarships to the Grammar School, as did John Steele, though he was at one time suspended from the Boys' School for disobedience. Also suspended for some time were Alfred Dance, Fred Dyson and C. Hopkins. They were usually re-instated after an apology and a promise not to repeat the misdemeanour. Considering the problems with disciplining large numbers of boys in the same room, these pupils must have been particularly disruptive.

Lateness and failure to complete home lessons were a common fault and innumerable boys were kept after school hours to do extra work. A few volunteered to come in to school early to learn extra subjects so that the Government Grant money was increased.

Mr. Gardner too had to work with the 'dull' and 'backward' children, still poorly prepared to enter the Boys' School. You can feel his frustration when he wrote in September 1887:

> *'The 4th St. are continually having spelling lessons, and yet this subject is very little better. Half of the boys seem incapable of retaining any difficult word for above twenty-four hours.'*

The same week, he is approached by a parent whose describes his son as:

> *'"Not quite the thing" and expressed a wish that he should learn but very little.'*

In December, the mother of one of the boys:

> *'came to the school and expressed a wish that he should be very leniently dealt with in his lessons owing to his defective intellect.'*

Although there were problems with spelling, when the whole school was tested in Arithmetic the following month, most of the Standards achieved results of between 91% and 96%, but with Standards 4 and 5 achieving only 72%. Mr. Gardner's frustration spilled over again in his entry for October 7th 1887:

> *'These two standards [i.e. 4 & 5] improve, (as far as examinations prove) not one whit, and repeatedly make the same mistakes, no matter what explanations are given & what punishments are meted out to them.'*

Even today, teachers will talk of 'good years' and 'bad years' when it seems a whole age group of children across schools seem to be particularly troublesome, or particularly bright. In South Warwickshire, with the eleven-plus system, this is reflected in the different scores required for acceptance into a Grammar School in different years.

Mr. Gardner must have been relieved to read the Inspector's Report for 1887:

> *'I am glad to find the promise of last year fulfilled and the school advancing so rapidly in efficiency. Order is very exact and Instruction generally much above the average.*

The 5th & 6th Standards are rather weak but the others pass a very good examination.
The attendance is improving.
The average attendance in the Boys' School must not be allowed again to exceed the accommodation reckoned at eight sq. feet for each child.'

Behaviour outside the classroom did not change much over 30 years. Although Mr. Phillip recorded very few instances of misbehaviour outside school hours, apart from a disinclination to do 'Home Lessons', before him, Mr. Sayce seemed constantly to be issuing cautions and lectures:

March 1863	*'Infants cautioned against throwing stones.'*
June 1863	*'Children cautioned against playing in the water & wetting their feet.'*
August 1863	*'Children lectured on fighting with each other.'*
February 1864	*'Children severely reprimanded for walking along neighbour's palisading. Children severely reprimanded for playing at bandy in the public street and for tearing sticks out of fences.'*
December 1865	*'Children admonished in using bad language to poor travellers.'*
March 1867	*'Children reprimanded for throwing snowballs.'*
January 1868	*'Children cautioned against loitering on the way from & to school.'*

Mr. Gardner recorded similar instances:

July 1887	*'Two boys W. Tarplee aged 12 and E. Rose aged 11 quarrelled and fought.'*
September 1887	*'Boys cautioned for stone-throwing.'*
November 1887	*'Samuel Hayes was punished "for insulting a man named Dudley as he was going by the school premises".'*

Only very occasionally was there worse behaviour:

July 1882	*'Having experienced so much of the lying habits & pilfering propensities of Wm. Maddon a workhouse boy & having found him guilty of abstracting certain money from a private drawer in my desk I (with the full concurrence of the Rev A H Williams, Chairman) felt it my bounden duty to expel the boy from my School.'*

March 1891   *'As William Stockton was coming to school this afternoon, he stole an orange from a tradesman's shop. I sent him in charge of an older lad to return the orange, & informed his parents.'*

April 1901   *'A boy (Albert Newton) stole a pinny from another boy and repeatedly denied it. Punished by a sharp caning.'*

Boys in 1900. Many of these seem to be about 11-12 (school leaving age).

Chapter 12

HOLIDAYS

Holidays seem to have been given for various reasons – some for no apparent reason. The following relates to the school year 1st July 1874 to 30th June 1875:

July 8th	half holiday [no reason given]
July 16th	whole day holiday [no reason given]
August 3rd	half holiday [no reason given]
August 7th	whole day holiday for Ragley Fete
August 14th to September 14th	Harvest holiday
October 6th	holiday for Alcester Statute Fair
October 12th	Stratford Fair
October 13th	second Alcester Fair [Runaway Mop]
November 20th	half holiday to prepare for the visit of Princess Christian
November 21st	half holiday for the Royal visit, which did not take place because of the poor weather
November 22nd	whole day holiday for the children to go to Ragley Hall to see the Royal Hunt [possibly as compensation for their missing out on the Church visit]
December 24th to January 11th	Christmas Holidays
March 26th	whole day holiday for Good Friday
March 29th	half holiday for Easter Monday
May 6th	half holiday for the Bishop's visit for the Confirmation Service in St. Nicholas' Church
May 17th – 21st	Whitsuntide Holidays
June 30th	half holiday [no reason given]

This was the last day of the school year and the new school year began on the following day, July 1st. In 1880, the dates of the school year were changed so that the year began on November 1st and ended on October 31st.

Although it was usual from the start to have a week or more as a Christmas Holiday, it was not until 1878 that the school was closed for a week for Easter.

Before that, whole or half day holidays were given on Good Friday and Easter Monday, though several days were given for Whitsuntide. The main school holiday was the Harvest Holiday, taking up four weeks during August and September. Again, from 1880 this was changed so that the school was closed from the middle / end of July for four weeks.

Other instances of extra holidays given are:

Aug. 2nd 1872   *'No School on Tuesday – Half Holiday on Thursday afternoon on account of the Choir Festival which was held in the Church.'*

Nov. 20th 1874   *'Gave half holiday in the afternoon in order to prepare the Schools by decorating & illuminating for the arrival of Prince & Princess Christian.'*

Nov. 21st   *'Gave half holiday on Wednesday as the children were requested to attend Church in order to do honour to Princess Christian on the occasion of her visiting it.'*

Nov. 22nd   *'Gave half holiday again on Thursday afternoon for the reason stated above as the Princess did not arrive yesterday owing to the unfavourable state of the weather.*
Gave holiday on Thursday as the school children were invited to Ragley Hall at 11 a.m. in order to see the Royal Hunt. Whilst there a number of buns were distributed amongst them.'

March 14th 1879   *'Gave Half Holiday on Thursday afternoon in honour of the Duke of Connaught's Marriage.'* [The Duke of Connaught was the seventh child of Queen Victoria. He married Princess Louise, daughter of Prince Frederick of Prussia.]

March 12th 1880   *'Gave a half holiday on Monday as the Bishop of Worcester was holding a Confirmation Service in the Alcester Church.'*

April 6th 1880   *'Gave Half Holiday in the afternoon on account of the South Warwickshire Election.'*

May 13th 1880   *'Gave a half holiday on Thursday Afternoon as Fawcett's Circus was in the Town.'*

It also became the custom to give half holidays after the school had been inspected both by Her Majesty's Inspector and the Diocesan Inspector.

Nov. 1884   *'Mr Milman H M I. visited & examined the school in the morning. Gave a half holiday in the afternoon.'*

This custom was observed by Miss Carter, then Miss Clark, in the Infants' School, and presumably by Mrs. Bates in the Girls' School.

Sometimes the school was closed for apparently trivial reasons:

Jan. 15th 1885   *'Children dismissed a little earlier during this week as the afternoons were very dark.'*

But we must remember that this was before the days of street lighting, and children often had to walk some distance on rough paths between school and home. Similarly, on dark mornings, attendance was not what it should have been.

In June 1885, Mr. Phillip *'Gave half holiday on Monday afternoon on account of the Alcester Athletic Sports.'*

A National holiday was declared for Queen Victoria's Golden Jubilee on June 20th 1887. Local celebrations took place on Tuesday June 21st. On June 8th Mr. Gardner *'Distributed free tickets for the "Jubilee Tea" among all those present'.* Unfortunately, what was intended as a day's holiday became for many children the whole week. Mr. Gardner had to close the school on the Wednesday as not enough boys were present, and although it re-opened on Thursday afternoon and Friday, few boys attended.

Reading between the lines, I feel Mr. Gardner became quite frustrated at the interruptions caused to the children's education by the number of holidays imposed upon the school by custom.

By the School Year 1889-90, there was a more regular pattern of terms and holidays, with fewer odd days being given, though this did not prevent a number of children, including Infants, absenting themselves to visit 'wild beast' shows, the circus and the monthly Cattle Sales.

Nov. 8th 1889	*'Gave holiday this afternoon.'*
Nov. 15th	*'Closed school for the day at 11.20 a.m. the registers having been marked at 9.10.'*
Dec. 10 – Jan. 6	**Christmas Holidays**
Feb. 18th	*'Closed Registers at 9.10, dispensed with the Scripture Lesson, and dismissed at 11.15 for the day, the majority of the boys wishing to attend the Sunday School Treat.'*
March 31st	*'The Scripture Examination took place to-day, concluding at 12.15. The usual half-holiday was given in the afternoon.'*
April 4 – 14	**Easter Holidays**
May 9th	*'Following the precedent of other years, holiday was given this afternoon in honour of the Bishop's visit to hold a Confirmation.'*

May 23rd – 30th **Whit-Week Holiday**

July 31st *'Broke up for the Harvest Holidays at 11.15 a.m., the Registers having been marked & closed by 9.10.'*

July 31 – Sept. 1st **Harvest Holidays – Four Weeks**

Oct. 7th *'Alcester mop takes place to-day, so the usual half-holiday was given.'*

Oct. 31st 1890 **End of School Year**

July 15th 1893 *'A holiday given on July 6th on account of the Royal Wedding.'* [This was the wedding of Prince George, Duke of York (later George V), to Princess Victoria Mary of Teck (later Queen Mary)]

Feb 23rd 1894 *'A half holiday given this day on account of the playgrounds being repaired.'*

June 22nd 1897 *'The school closed on Jubilee Day.'* [This was Queen Victoria's Diamond Jubilee.]

May 25 1900 *'A holiday given on Thursday (May 24th) in honour of the Queen's Birthday.'* [In later years 24th May was celebrated as Empire Day – I remember a rhyme we sang at school in the 1950s – '24th of May, Empire Day, if we don't have a holiday, we'll all run away.']

Alcester Sunday School Picnic (date unknown).

Aug 1st 1901	*'An extra holiday granted by the Managers, as one of the boys (Evan Gardner) had gained a County Scholarship.'*
June 2nd 1902	*'A holiday given in commemoration of peace being declared after the war in South Africa'* [also referred to as the Second Boer War – 1899-1902.]
June 24th 1902	*'Close school this day (Tuesday) for the Coronation Festivities.'*
June 25th	*'Owing to the postponement of the Coronation we decided to open school this morning and close until Monday next, at noon today Wednesday.'* [Although Queen Victoria had died in January 1901, the Coronation of Edward VII was not arranged until 26th June 1902. Unfortunately he had to undergo an emergency operation for appendicitis and his Coronation was re-scheduled for August 9th.]
July 1902	*'A holiday given on July 11th in commemoration of three County Scholarships gained by two boys and a girl belonging to the school.'*

Chapter 13

SALARIES

When setting up the 'new' Schools in 1871, it was decided to retain the existing staff of Mr. James Sayce and Miss Lucy Walsingham. Mr. Sayce was to receive a fixed salary for twelve months of £60 and Miss Walsingham to receive £20, '*in addition to which each to receive one third of the Government grant and one third of the pence earned in their respective Schools.*'

In February 1871, the Managers appointed Mrs. Fanny Bates, a widow from Stourton, Shipston-on-Stour to the post of Mistress of the Girls' School. She was offered a salary of £30 per annum, plus one third of the Government Grant (This amount was dependent on the performance of the children at the annual Inspection by Her Majesty's Inspector), plus one third of the school pence (This amount was dependent on pupil attendance), giving an expected annual total of £60.

For her extra work in covering the Boys' School between the dismissal of Mr. Sayce in October 1871 and the arrival of Mr. Phillip in January 1872, Mrs. Bates was awarded an additional Seven Pounds Ten Shillings; and her daughter received One Pound '*for the assistance rendered to her Mother in the same period*'.

Salaries were negotiable, and teachers applied to the Managers annually for an increase.

In 1876, Alice Hoy completed her apprenticeship in the Girls' School, and was offered '*the post as Assistant Mistress in the Girls' and Infants' Schools at a commencing salary of £30*'.

In 1881, the Managers were trying to find a suitable teacher with '*special infant training*' to run the Infants' School. Eventually, after turning down several unsuitable candidates, they appointed Miss M.A. Carter, who had been trained at Whitelands Training College. This College had been set up in Whitelands House, Kings Road, Chelsea in 1841 specifically for training women as teachers. She received a starting salary of £70 per annum.

In 1897:

Boys' School – Mr. Gardner (Master), £120; Mr. Whiting (Assistant), £55; Mrs. Gardner (Assistant), £50 per annum.

Girls' School – Mrs. Bates (Mistress), £92; Miss Edwin (Assistant), £50; Miss Tunnicliffe (Assistant), £35 per annum.

Infants' School – Miss Clark (Mistress), £85; Miss Cooper (Assistant), £40; Miss Gray (Assistant), £40 per annum.

In 1899, Mary Ann Thornley succeeded Mrs. Bates. Although Mr. Gardner and Miss Clark were receiving the same amounts Miss Thornley's salary was £82 per annum. In 1904, the annual salaries were recorded as follows:

<u>Boys' School</u>

Mr. Gardner	120.0.0
Mrs. Gardner	65.0.0
Mr. W.J. Slade	65.0.0

<u>Girls' School</u>

Miss Thornley	80.0.0
Miss Chambers	40.0.0
Miss Bates	30.0.0
K. Coley (Monitress)	8.0.0

<u>Infants' School</u>

Miss Clark	90.0.0
Miss Cooper	45.0.0
Miss Morris	45.0.0

It is obvious from the figures shown throughout that 'equal pay for equal work' was unheard of and men were paid quite a lot more money than women for doing similar work.

Chapter 14

ODDS AND ENDS

1866 *March*   'Cattle plague.
    April   School at Arrow opened – approximately 20 children left
        Alcester to go the new school.
    July   Many children absent for a trial trip on the new railway.
    September   The Alcester Railway opened officially.
    November   Children were cautioned against the use of gunpowder!

1867 *November*   Three children dead from Scarlet Fever.

1868 *December*   'The Night school closed till after Xmas – the scholars busy in
        the factories in preparing orders for Christmas.'

1869 *April*   Many children, as well as staff, are sick with the fever.'

1870 *Annual Report – '...ventilation not good. The smell in the Infants School
was very offensive. The room was overcrowded & yet there are scores of
children growing up un-educated; the school rooms should be enlarged and
class rooms added without delay.'* According to Mr Sayce, *'The smell in the
Infant school was caused by a gardener manuring his land.'*

*'George Day died after a few hours sickness on Sunday, yesterday. A clean
boy.'*

1871 July 3rd   'James Parker sick.'
    July 24th   'James Cale absent – broke his thigh.'
    Aug 1st   'James Parker died.'

1872 Jan 8th   'During the week the children were arranged into classes
        according to their attainments. The school fees have been
        raised so that they now are 3d per week for the first child
        in a family & 2d for each of the remainder in the same
        family – 2d per week for all Factory children & 6d per week

for children whose parents are employers of labour or
superior tradesmen.'

1873   Sept   'Reopened the School in the Town Hall along with the Girls
            & Infants as the Schoolrooms are being enlarged.'

      Oct   'Still at the Town Hall. There being only 6 desks for all the
            children very few could write in Copy Books. Found the room
            very close & children noisy.'

      Nov   'Brought the Boys down from the Town Hall to their new
            room on Monday. The children were still unable to write in
            Copy Books as the new ink wells have not yet arrived.'

      Dec   'The new ink wells arrived this week.'

1874   Dec 29th   'The Marquis of Hertford distributed the prizes to the
             successful competitors in the Corn Exchange in the following
             order:

Scripture

1st Class.	Wesley Gittus	An Album
	William Stanley – commended	Pen
2nd Class.	Albt Cull	Writing Case
3rd Class.	Matthew Ellins	Paint Box
	William John Haywood – commended	

Dictation & Arithmetic

1st Class.	Wesley Gittus	
	William Stanley	Writing Case
2nd Class.	Thomas Jobson	Knife
	Albert Cull	Pencil
3rd Class.	Alex Moore	Box & Pencils.'

1875   'Admitted Alfred Ellins who has hitherto attended a Dame school & though
nearly 8 years of age yet he can do little more than form strokes on a slate.'

1876   'Weekly average 68.7 being the largest of any during the present School year.
This increase is partly owing to the fact that the Agricultural Children's Act
was brought into operation in this country a week or two ago; the result of
this is the fourth class is now full to overflowing by children from 8 to 11
years of age, many of whom scarcely know their letters.'

1877 *'The Rev A H Williams & Mr. Averill visited the school in order to present a shilling [5p] to each boy who passed in 3 subjects & 8d to each who passed in 2 subjects.'*

1878 *'Days very short. Children much inclined to be late in attendance.'*

1879 *'Wrote to J D B Faber Esq H M I asking for permission to change the Geo: of the 1st class from America to Asia or Asia & Africa.*
Received the reply on Thursday stating that the request could not be granted.'

1880 March 11th *'Three medical gentlemen... together with Mr. Gander the Nuisance Inspector, attended the school & examined all the children to see if any are suffering from infectious diseases of any kind the result of which was that several were sent home & are not to be allowed to return without a Medical Certificate.'*

1881 Jan 16th *'Gave half holiday in the afternoon in order to attend the opening service of the new organ which has just been placed in the Church.'*

1882 The Managers were ordered By H.M. Inspector that *'all children to be passed into the upper schools at 6 years irrespective of their proficiency'*. The Managers were unhappy with this decision and wrote to the Education Department asking *'whether the age limit might not in some cases be allowed to give place to a consideration of efficiency – or in many cases where the children did not know their letters the system of the Infants School would be more suited to their want.'*

1883 *'Gave half holiday on Friday afternoon as the Odd Fellows were holding their Anniversary Dinner in the Corn Exchange.'*

'Gave two boys six strokes of the cane for copying.'

1884 *'a door was ordered to be put on the lavatory in the Girls' yard.'*
'Many children late this week as the mornings are dark.'

1885 *'Attendance very irregular this week as many of the boys have been engaged currant picking.'*

1886 *'About half-a-dozen children are suffering from ulcerated throats.'*

1887   *'Admitted a new boy named George Crowe aged six. He has never been to school before, and in consequence knows nothing.'*

'Just before nine o'clock two boys W. Tarplee aged 12 and E. Rose aged 11 quarrelled and fought. Immediately after parting them, I punished Tarplee for again striking Rose. The former still proved obdurate and sulky when school work began, and I was again forced to use the cane, this time more severely.'

1888   *'The Chairman reported that HM Inspectors required a group of desks to be substituted for one of the galleries in the Infant School & submitted sketches. The desks were ordered.'*

1889   *'William Smith in 5th Standard returned to School this week after an absence of eleven weeks including holidays. He has made 122 attendances only all the year.'*

1890   *'Re-admitted Brandon Lewis who has recently been attending the Catholic School. His fee has been raised from 3d to 4d by order of the Managers, who have adopted this plan to discourage the system of flitting from one school to another.'*

1891   *'The father of Arthur Shuff has requested me to treat his son leniently. The latter was bitten by a dog some time ago & has not yet recovered from the shock.'*

1892   Jan 11th   *'Reopened school only 61 children present owing to a deep snow.'*
             Feb 22nd   *'The attendance this week is much lower owing to a very heavy fall of snow.'*

1893   *'The Chairman submitted the Report after the visit of HM Inspectors which was altogether satisfactory. Each School obtained the "Excellent" Merit Grade.'*

1894   *'A half holiday given this day on account of the playgrounds being repaired. The children have had extra marching lessons this week owing to the extremely cold weather.'*

1895   *'The Report of HM Inspector was submitted & considered. All the Departments were awarded the "Excellent" Merit Grant. .... Total 317.15.6 This was reduced on account of insufficient staff ... and the sum received was £303.15.6.'*

1896 *'The average attendance of the past year was lower by 15 owing to an epidemic in the spring.'*

1897 *'Resolved that the Schools have the usual week's holiday and a Jubilee holiday* [Queen Victoria's Diamond Jubilee] *on June 22.... The School holidays were fixed from July 29 to Aug 30.'*

1898 *'Mr. T.H. Smith reported that his father* [Mr T.L. Smith] *had left by will £100 free of duty to be paid to the Treasurer of the Alcester Nat[ional] Schools, if they were Church of England Schools at the time of his death.'*

1899 *'An application from Mrs Davis, Salt Box Row undertaking to clean the Schools ... (finding her own materials) at 10/- per week was accepted.'*
Mr Henderson drew out a list of rules:

'Rules for Care-takers

Sweep out 3 schools, classrooms, porches & offices every afternoon when schools have been open.
Dust all schools & classrooms every morning & light fires (8) if necessary.
Scrub out school, one porch & one classroom every week.
Scrub all offices every week.
Find all brooms, dusters etc.
Clean windows – in & out – of one school etc each week.
Scrub all inside walls once a quarter.
Keep office pans [toilet bowls] *clean.*
Black grates every week & whiten hearth stones.
These duties to apply to the Day Schools only.'

1900

July *'Mr Gothard the Secretary was directed to communicate with Mr Johnson of Headless Cross asking him to inspect the School Offices* [toilets] *& advise as to their reconstruction on the Automatic Flush System.'*

Aug. *'The estimated expenditure was considered beyond the means at the disposal of the Managers & the question was postponed.'*

June 22nd, 1897.

1901 '*The Attendance registers were quite destroyed by the recent Flood (Dec 31st 1900). The attendances (which had been marked in red ink) were undecipherable.*'

'*On the proposition of the Chairman seconded by Mr Gothard a clock of the value of 19/6 was granted for the Boys' School.*'

1902 March '*The Chairman reported that the Infants' School had been closed for a week in consequence of the illness of Misses Clarke, Cooper & Gray.*'

June '*Coronation songs substituted for other songs and recitations. Conversational Lesson on the Declaration of Peace and on the Coronation taken with the two upper classes.*'

1903 The final meeting of the Managers under the old regime was recorded thus: '*A Meeting of the Managers was called for Friday June 12 1903 at 5pm. But the Rector only being present no business could be done – The teachers were in attendance with their reports.*'

INDEX OF NAMES